NEW LIFE

in 3 Priorities of

TRIUMPH

Transformation ABC in

The Kingdom of God.

By José E. Espinoza © 2025

José E. Espinoza

Dedication

To a Human Being Redeemed to Enter the Kingdom of God, with the Purpose to take the Rightful Royal Position During Life in Planet Earth.

-   *José E. Espinoza*

José E. Espinoza

NEW LIFE   In 3 Priorities of TRIUMPH

Table of Contents

NEW LIFE   In 3 Priorities of   TRIUMPH

José E. Espinoza

<u>**Introduction**</u>

Imagine for a moment that you've just stepped into **a new chapter of your life**—one filled with <u>hope</u>, <u>purpose</u>, and the promise of <u>transformation</u>. You may be a young adult who has recently encountered the message of Jesus, or perhaps someone <u>longing for a fresh start through faith in Jesus Christ seeking and entering the Kingdom of God</u>. The excitement of this spiritual awakening is undeniable, yet it's often accompanied by a cascade of questions: Where do I begin? How can I grow closer to God? What does **authentic adoration, honoring and worship to God** really mean? Is prayer truly as powerful as people say? If any of these thoughts resonate with you, you're not alone. **This book is for you**—<u>the seeker, **the new believer**</u>, the young adult eager <u>to build something lasting with God</u>.

Entering a relationship with God isn't about memorizing religious routines or performing rituals out of obligation. It's about discovering a connection so **real and personal** it begins to shape everything you do. But here's the truth: many start their faith journey with excitement, but over time, daily pressures, doubts, and even boredom can creep in. That's normal—spiritual growth doesn't happen overnight, nor does it come without effort. Yet within every person lies a yearning for deeper meaning, a desire to encounter God not just on Sundays, but every single day. This is where the adventure of adoration and prayer begins.

Let's talk about 'Adoration/Worship'—not as a chore or a box to check off, but as the heartbeat of your new life with God. Adoration/Worship is more than music or singing in church; it's the way you respond to the greatness and love of your Creator. Think of it as showing appreciation to someone who continually pours goodness into your life. **True adoration/worship** opens a pathway to experiencing God's presence, transforming ordinary routines into moments of awe and gratitude. This change doesn't require perfection—it only asks for honesty. When you approach God from a place of sincerity, admitting your needs, struggles, and hopes, that's when **real transformation takes place**. Worship, then, becomes the sturdy foundation upon which every other part of your spiritual journey is built.

Yet, **genuine adoration/worship** cannot thrive without <u>prayer</u>. **<u>Prayer</u>** <u>is the conversation that turns belief into relationship</u>. It's not reserved for the 'super spiritual' or those with eloquent words—**it's for <u>anyone willing to talk with God</u> honestly**. Some days, prayer will feel like pouring your heart out. Other days, it may be quiet and reflective. Sometimes, you'll have a list of questions or requests; at other times, you'll simply sit in silence, listening. No matter the shape it takes, **prayer is how you invite God into your world**, share your burdens, and receive His direction. And when life gets hard—as it inevitably does—<u>prayer is the safe space</u> where fears are calmed and courage is restored.

Why start with adoration and prayer? Because <u>these two practices align your heart and mind with what matters most</u>. They cut through distractions and anxieties, turning your attention to God's promises instead of your problems. Many people struggle with consistency, wondering why their faith feels shallow or why God seems distant. But by embedding adoration/worship and prayer into your routine, you begin to experience faith as a living, breathing relationship rather than an abstract idea. This shift leads to greater resilience, joy, and peace—qualities we desperately need in today's chaotic world.

But there's **another reason** these basics are so essential: they help you develop a 'kingdom of God' mindset. Following Jesus isn't just about personal comfort; it's about stepping into a bigger story. **God invites you to see life from a new perspective**—to make decisions, form habits, and pursue ambitions shaped by eternal values, not just cultural trends. **When you put God's priorities first**, you discover a sense of purpose that outlasts fleeting happiness. Every act of kindness, every moment spent **seeking God's will**, becomes part of something bigger—a movement of love and justice that brings light into dark places.

Of course, any honest exploration of faith must recognize the obstacles ahead. There will be seasons when worship feels dry, when prayers seem unanswered, when doubts threaten to take over. Sometimes it will be tempting to give up, to slip back into old habits or tune out God's voice amid life's noise. But here's the encouragement you need: **you're not meant to tackle these challenges alone**. The Christian journey is not a solo expedition. Community—with fellow believers who <u>support, encourage</u>, and learn alongside you—is one of God's greatest gifts. It's in community where you can ask tough questions, <u>celebrate victories</u>, and lean on the strength of others when yours is running low.

Within this family of faith, you'll also encounter the **authority and wisdom of scripture. <u>The Bible</u>** isn't just a dusty rulebook—<u>it's God's invitation into His story</u>. Its teachings <u>provide clarity</u> in confusion, <u>offer hope</u> in despair, and <u>challenge you to live courageously</u>. As you read its pages, you'll uncover **promises** that anchor you during storms, **truths** <u>that inspire action</u>, and **practical guidance** for everyday living. <u>Trusting the Bible</u> means <u>you always have a compass</u>—no matter how unpredictable the journey ahead.

And what about the **Holy Spirit**? If this sounds mysterious, you're right to be curious. **The Holy Spirit <u>is God present</u>** and <u>active in your daily life</u>—**comforting, guiding, and empowering** you <u>to make choices that reflect Christ</u>. Through the Spirit, ordinary moments become opportunities for extraordinary encounters. Whether it's finding <u>wisdom</u> in a tough decision, <u>comfort</u> in sorrow, or

<u>courage</u> to serve others, **The Holy Spirit** <u>equips you for every step</u> of <u>your faith walk</u>.

As you travel deeper into <u>this book</u>, you'll find practical steps and real-life examples to help weave **ADORATION/*WORSHIP*** and **PRAYER** into your daily routine. You'll discover how to overcome distractions, **cultivate a <u>kingdom of God</u> perspective**, adopting **The BIBLE** as ***God's living word* <u>and trustworthy promises</u>**, and enter into a vibrant, **HOLY SPIRIT Connected**-led community life. Each chapter is designed to meet you where you are—whether you're full of questions, fresh with enthusiasm, or in need of reassurance. You'll be challenged to move beyond surface-level beliefs, to embrace a lifestyle of ongoing devotion, and to let your personal story become part of God's unfolding plan for the world.

A meaningful relationship with God starts with a willing heart. You don't need special qualifications, a perfect background, or all the answers. **You only need openness**—a readiness to engage in genuine adoration/worship to The True Loving God, honest prayer to/with The Loving Father and King of kings, and intentional community guided by The Holy Spirit. The journey won't always be easy. There will be setbacks and detours. But as you keep taking intentional steps, you'll find yourself growing in ways you never thought possible. You'll gain strength for trials, compassion for others, and a sense of purpose that infuses every part of your life.

Consider this introduction both an invitation and a roadmap. Whether you've just said yes to Jesus, are searching for deeper meaning, or are looking to revitalize your faith, you belong here. The adventure that awaits is richer than anything the world alone can offer. Step forward—arms open, heart expectant—and allow adoration/worship, prayer, the bible and The Holy Spirit to lead you toward the **fullness of life** God has planned for you. Your story is only beginning, and the best is yet to come.

José E. Espinoza

Part 1:

Adoration and Prayer

Chapter 1:

ADORATION/Worship to <u>Our</u> <u>Father God</u>

As Primary Foundation of Faith

Have you ever found yourself yearning for a **deeper connection**, feeling that the routine of life has left you somewhat detached from the spiritual fulfillment you seek? Many begin their journey of faith with enthusiasm, yet as they navigate daily challenges, maintaining an authentic and vibrant relationship with God can become challenging. It's easy to fall into the rhythm of rituals, where worship feels more like a task to tick off than a profound encounter with the Divine Loving Father-King of kings and Lord of lords. In seeking to nurture this sincere connection, one might wonder how worship can transcend these limitations, fostering a true transformation within. Furthermore, <u>if you have truly embraced The Savior</u>, **Jesus of Nazareth**, in your heart as The Christ—<u>the mediator and redeemer of your life</u>, thus entering the Kingdom of

. it is natural for your spirit to yearn to honor, adore, and worship Him as such loving <u>Sovereign Father God</u>. This spiritual inclination also extends to a sincere **desire to pray effectively**, seeking to <u>understand and fulfill His will</u>.

In this chapter, we will explore why **genuine Adoration &/or worship** is <u>essential for personal faith and growth</u>, examining the importance of authenticity and the transformative power it holds when integrated into everyday life. We will delve into overcoming obstacles that hinder heartfelt worship, guiding believers toward <u>a life illuminated by joy and victory in alignment with God's kingdom</u>.

NEW LIFE   In 3 Priorities of TRIUMPH

Authentic Transformation when you Adore or Worship

Sincerity in worship plays a vital role in a believer's spiritual journey, knitting together the threads of faith, **personal growth**, and genuine **connection with God**. Real worship transcends spoken words, inviting believers to embrace an intimate engagement with God that adopt a deeper relationship. It is this heartfelt engagement that prompts believers to open up, allowing God's transformative work to occur in their lives. By engaging in a personal experience, believers set the stage for spiritual growth that is both profound and life-altering.

At the core of genuine adoration or worship is the departure from mere rituals. Instead of viewing worship as a rote exercise, sincere believers find meaning in every act, transforming conventional practices into significant expressions of faith. Creativity has a unique role here, offering believers the opportunity to express their devotion in diverse and enriching ways. Whether through song, prayer, or silent meditation, each act reflects a personalized approach to worship. Honesty becomes crucial in this endeavor. As believers recognize their failings and seek grace, they invite authentic spiritual growth into their lives.

Adoration or worship stands as an eloquent expression of love and gratitude, towards our loving heavenly Father, Mighty God, and King of kings, enriching not only individual spiritual journeys, but also fortifying a sense of community among believers, within the royal family of the Kingdom of Heaven on Earth. By worshiping together, individuals can experience an enhanced sense of connectivity, a crucial element in understanding and internalizing God's will and purpose for their lives. This community connection serves as both a foundation and a support system for personal transformation. Engaging in worship allows believers to explore humility, positioning themselves as servants both to God and one another, encouraging acts of kindness and fostering a unifying spirit within the community.

Reflecting on scripture's insights into worship, such as those in **Romans 12:1-2** and **John 4:23-24**, (The Gospel of <u>John 4:23</u> states; **"But the hour cometh, and now is, when the true worshippers shall <u>WORSHIP</u> The Father <u>in spirit</u> and <u>in truth;</u> for The Father seeketh such**

to worship Him". -KJV.). Believers find that true worship involves offering one's entire being to God, transcending physical expressions and diving into spiritual sincerity and authenticity. (Wilson, 2024; Topical Bible: Spiritual Worship Today, 2025). Aligning with the truth of **God's Word ensures that this worship is based on divine revelation** rather than human traditions.

Adoration and/or Worship, thus, becomes not just a momentary event but an ongoing life practice. It seeps into daily thoughts, actions, and decisions, reflecting one's values and beliefs. Understanding worship as a lifestyle promotes mindfulness and a deeper awareness of God's presence in every aspect of existence. **More than a Sunday morning routine**, it is a continuous act of surrender and adoration, leading to everyday choices that mirror an unwavering commitment to God's will.

For instance, let's consider a believer (or even you in this case) grappling with stress and uncertainty at work. Instead of fostering anxiety, they/you may turn to worship as a means of finding peace and direction. By inviting God into your or their situation through genuine adoration or worship, you or any believer, align the perspective, seeking divine guidance rather than relying solely on our own understanding. In doing so, we experience God's calming presence, which shifts our mindset from one of turmoil to one of trust and assurance. This shift in perspective is indicative of worship's transformative power, revealing deeper insights into God's will and often leading to more thoughtful, godly decision-making.

The transformational journey through adoring and/or worship challenges you and any believers to step away from the distractions of modern life, the temptations of entertainment, and the reduction of worship to mere performance. (Topical Bible: Spiritual Worship Today, 2025). By focusing instead on disciplined spiritual practices grounded in prayer and scripture, believers ensure their worship remains genuine and God-centered. Such a disciplined approach counteracts external noise and refines one's spiritual focus, leading to greater spiritual clarity and alignment with God's desires.

Worship's transformative nature brings about a renewed perspective. As believers engage in true adoration/worship, they set aside worldly values, opting instead to align with God's eternal perspective. (Wilson, 2024). This alignment allows them to see themselves and others through the lenses of love, forgiveness, and grace. It challenges existing negative thought patterns, replacing them with God's truth, fostering feelings of hope, faith, and confidence in divine promises.

By nurturing a worship-centered life, believers also open themselves to discernment. A heart tuned to heaven can **easily detect God's voice and direction in everyday life.** (Topical Bible: Spiritual Worship Today, 2025). This intimate space of worship becomes an incubator for receiving **divine guidance**, steering believers away from self-reliance and inviting trust and **confidence in God's wisdom**. Such discernment often brings peace and assurance, reinforcing believers' confidence as they navigate life's complexities.

Ultimately, adoration/worship is a journey—a continuous process that encourages believers to participate fully, to embody the love and grace they receive in their day-to-day interactions. It calls for a mindset of servitude, promoting humility, which naturally extends into acts of kindness, charity, and unity within the community. This active servitude reflects a deep understanding of worship's purpose, reinforcing its role as a crucial component of the faith journey.

Moving forward, embracing adoration/worship as a lifestyle involves integrating it into the mundane and extraordinary, continuously reflecting God's values in every action taken. As this journey unfolds, believers live with a heightened awareness of God's presence, guiding their choices and actions in pursuit of a life that resonates with divine will. This perpetual engagement opens the door to further spiritual growth, positioning worship not just as an isolated experience but as a foundational element that enriches the entirety of a believer's life.

Adoration/Worship as a Lifestyle <u>Choice</u>

Authenticity in adoration/worship transforms it from a mere act into a state of being, transcending traditional parameters and fostering a profound personal transformation. It's about sincerity, where actions speak louder than words, and rituals evolve into meaningful expressions of faith. This sincerity paves the way for growth and transformation, engaging believers on a deeper level that binds the ordinary moments of life with spiritual significance.

Worship isn't just for Sunday mornings in a church pew; it becomes a lifestyle when integrated seamlessly into daily existence. It molds a path where every action, thought, and decision reflects the values and beliefs held by the individual. Think of worship as the continuous hum of a melody that plays throughout the day, influencing behaviors and thoughts subtly yet profoundly. The choice to embrace worship as a lifestyle infuses life with a consistent awareness of God's presence, guiding every step made.

Envision the concept of constant engagement with God. It might begin with a morning prayer but extend to moments of gratitude at mealtimes, finding peace during a stressful commute, or offering silent thanks for small mercies throughout the day. This ongoing conversation with God encourages a deeper awareness of divine presence in everyday life. Staying mindful that worship permeates the mundane transforms each trivial task into a reflection of praise and acknowledgment of a higher power.

Discipline plays a pivotal role in embedding worship into daily life. It's all too easy to let distractions veer one off course; hence, intentionality becomes essential. Structuring time for quiet reflection or prayer, even amidst busy schedules, can be crucial. Integrating worship into the routine may require setting reminders to pause during the day, engage in spiritual reading, or simply enjoy nature as an act of appreciation. Community becomes vital here. Having a network of fellow believers offers accountability, encouragement, and shared spiritual support. Gathering with others who share similar values creates a safe space for practicing worship in diverse forms, providing strength, especially in challenging times. The power of fellowship aids in grounding faith, supporting spiritual reinforcement, and ensuring regularity in one's worship practice. (Cullum, 2024).

A lifestyle steeped in Adoration/worship fosters **consistent spiritual growth and maturity. Over time**, the steady rhythm of daily devotion promotes emotional and spiritual resilience. Engaging regularly with God and incorporating biblical principles into life broadens understanding and insight into theological concepts, enhancing one's spiritual journey. The act of consistent worship challenges believers to delve deeper, nurturing spiritual and emotional development that builds robustness against life's trials. As faith deepens, so does the capacity to handle adversity, drawing strength from a well of spiritual resources cultivated through daily adoration and worship practices. (NGANYU, 2025).

Worshiping daily isn't only about personal growth; it generates an aura of gratitude, positivity, and encouragement in personal and communal relationships. When worship forms part of every interaction, it lifts the atmosphere, encouraging others around to pursue their spiritual fullness. Acts of kindness, generosity, and empathy become expressions of worshipful living, enriching lives beyond one's own. Practicing gratitude consistently, a core aspect of worship, creates positivity that inspires those around us, encouraging them to see God's work in everyday life. This pervasive sense of appreciation shifts perspectives in interactions and fosters communities built around care and spiritual fulfillment.

Consider the example of someone who starts their day with a simple prayer of gratitude, carries a short scripture in their pocket for inspiration, and consciously decides to offer a silent prayer for each person they encounter. Their actions reflect their commitment to worship, influencing their thoughts and behaviors, and ultimately, everyone they interact with feels the echo of their faith. Such tangible examples of worship in daily life help demystify the concept, making it relatable and achievable irrespective of one's circumstances.

As adoration/worship becomes ingrained within daily routines, it becomes vital to acknowledge the challenges that can disrupt consistency. There are times when sustaining a worshipful life feels like pushing against an insurmountable wall. Stress, distractions, and doubts can cloud one's path, making worship seem distant or irrelevant. Here lies the importance of anticipating these obstacles and developing strategies to overcome them. Preparing ourselves with flexible strategies ensures that adoration/worship practices remain fluid and adaptable, even when circumstances demand flexibility.

These strategies might include setting realistic goals for spiritual activities, seeking guidance from faith leaders, or engaging in community gatherings that provide spiritual sustenance and support. Overcoming such hurdles not only enriches the personal worship experience but strengthens the community through shared struggles and mutual encouragement. In these moments of challenge, believers redefine the boundaries of worship, ensuring that it remains genuine and meaningful at all times.

As one delves deeper into a lifestyle of adoration/worship, remember that the fusion of everyday life and spirituality nurtures a harmonious, joyful existence. Worship becomes liberating, a source of eternal strength and peace, and every step taken resonates with purpose and fulfillment. Prepare to explore the common obstacles faced in this spiritual journey, as identifying these allows believers to navigate challenges efficiently, keeping the path of worship open and vibrant. When traditional norms fade into the background, authentic engagement emerges, crafted by personal growth and interwoven with faith, leading to a more fulfilling spiritual adventure. (Cullum, 2024).

Overcoming Challenges in Adoration/Worship

Traditional worship rituals often risk becoming routine, which can make personal engagement feel limited and uninspired. You might find that your worship feels more like a series of actions than a meaningful interaction with God. By adopting creative approaches, you can transform adoration/worship into a vibrant, authentic experience that fosters deeper emotional connections with God. Consider how your adoration/worship practice can be a consistent part of your daily life, integrated with continuous and mindful engagement.

When adoration/worship becomes stale, exploring diverse expressions can breathe new life into your experience. For example, incorporating storytelling or sharing personal testimonies during worship can make it more relatable and personal, as suggested by Foster. (2020). This type of engagement invites authenticity and encourages vulnerability, strengthening your connection with God and each other. (Foster, 2020).

Distractions during worship challenge your ability to focus and engage meaningfully. Identifying common distractions is the first step towards overcoming them. One effective mindfulness technique involves setting aside designated quiet times without digital interruptions, allowing you to fully immerse yourself in worship. Integrating music or art, as highlighted in various team-building activities. (Mwema, 2024), offers another layer of enrichment, allowing creative expressions to enhance your communion with God.

Consider **creating a dedicated adoration/worship space at home**. This space doesn't have to be elaborate; even a small corner in your humble residence can be effective. By associating this space with your spiritual practice, you subconsciously prepare your mind for worship when you enter it. Regular community fellowship also plays a critical role in maintaining your adoration/worship practice, offering encouragement and accountability that reinforces your spiritual journey.

A structured approach to overcoming distractions involves these actionable steps. First, recognize what commonly pulls your attention away during adoration/worship. This could be anything from intrusive thoughts to external noise. Once identified, develop a personalized plan to address these distractions. For instance, if digital distractions are your primary hurdle, consider leaving your phone in a different room or using apps designed to minimize interruptions. The key is to consistently practice this plan daily. Over time, this discipline fosters a habit of focused adoration/worship, enhancing your spiritual experience.

Sharing these practices within your community strengthens your efforts. A shared commitment to overcoming challenges creates a supportive environment where everyone can thrive together. Engaging in regular discussions about adoration/worship practices not only offers new perspectives but also deepens communal bonds.

A vital component of engaging adoration/worship involves exploring various styles and expressions. Drawing from the idea of hosting a creative worship night, (Mwema, 2024), you might experiment with spoken word of the psalms, singing a praising son, or through the arts of playing a musical instrument, to diversify your worship experience. These forms of expression facilitate a break from routine, sparking creativity and collective participation.

NEW LIFE   In 3 Priorities of TRIUMPH

Maintaining a lifestyle of continuous adoration/worship aligns with **living out a victorious and triumphant life in God's Kingdom**. This involves integrating worship into every aspect of life, not just within designated times or spaces. Close your day with a moment of reflection or thanksgiving to cultivate gratitude and awareness of God's presence throughout your daily activities.

By being intentional about your adoration/worship practices, you lay the groundwork for a **deeper relationship with God**. Embrace the idea that **worship can rejuvenate** when it involves a variety of expressions and consistent practice. The result is not just a richer worship life, but a fuller, more authentic expression of faith that shines through your daily actions.

Consistent adoration/worship practices contribute to a community that values spiritual and emotional health, promoting a culture of understanding and support. As you pursue this lifestyle of continuous adoration/worship, be mindful of how each step contributes to the journey, fostering joy and resilience.

Your practice transforms when you overcome obstacles and embrace varied expressions. Engage sincerely, knowing that every moment in worship is an opportunity for growth and connection with God's presence. Keep exploring, experimenting, and sharing, as these actions not only enrich your adoration/worship but also sustain a community rich in faith and love.

Keeping adoration/worship fresh and meaningful requires creativity and adaptability. Use the insights gained from fostering vulnerability and **emotional intelligence** to inspire genuine worship experiences. Focus on how adoration/worship connects to your daily life, creating a seamless and ongoing dialogue with God that transcends any gathering. By doing so, you invite a **profound transformation** in your adoration/worship practices that resonates through every aspect of your life, <u>grounding you in a faith that is vibrant, authentic, and deeply fulfilling</u>.

NEW LIFE   In 3 Priorities of TRIUMPH

Summary and Reflections

In the journey of **cultivating genuine adoration/worship toward our Heavenly Father**, we've explored how sincerity and authenticity can transform routine acts into profound expressions of faith. Now that we know this, we can begin to integrate adoration and/or worship into every facet of our lives, allowing it to guide our thoughts, actions, and decisions. This lifestyle choice not only **enhances personal spiritual growth** but also strengthens community bonds, encouraging acts of kindness and unity. As young believers or newcomers seeking deeper connections with God, embracing a worship-centered life reveals pathways to **joy, peace, and divine purpose**. Through creativity and mindfulness, we are invited to overcome obstacles, ensuring our worship remains a vibrant and **meaningful dialogue with God**. By infusing worship into everyday moments, we open ourselves to continuous transformation, adopting resilience and clarity in alignment with our Father God's eternal perspective.

José E. Espinoza

Reference List

Cullum, B. (2024, August 19). *Harvest Counseling & Wellness.* Harvest Counseling & Wellness. https://www.harvestcounselingandwellness.com/blog/faith-focused-therapy

Leading with Compassion: Addressing Mental Health in Worship Leadership – jubileeschool.org. (2024, August 26). Jubileeschool.org. https://jubileeschool.org/leading-with-compassion-addressing-mental-health-in-worship-leadership/

Mwema, A. (2024, December 18). *Worship Team Building Activities for Unity and Connection.* Andrewmwema.com. https://www.andrewmwema.com/worship-team-building-activities-to-strengthen-unity-and-connection

NGANYU, G. N. (2025, January 31). *THEOLOGICAL AND PSYCHOLOGICAL INTEGRATION IN CHRISTIAN PSYCHOTHERAPY: A CRITICAL REVIEW OF THE LITERATURE AND IMPLICATIONS FOR CHURCH-BASED PRACTICE.* Greener Journal of Social Sciences; Greener Journals. https://doi.org/10.15580/gjss.2025.1.022525031

Topical Bible: Spiritual Worship Today. (2025). Biblehub.com. https://biblehub.com/topical/s/spiritual_worship_today.htm

Wilson, A. (2024, April 16). *6 Rewards of True Worship: Understanding Spirit and Truth in John.* God Is a Rewarder. https://godrewarder.com/understanding-spirit-and-truth/

Chapter 2:

PRAYER; Power & Practice

Connecting with God through prayer (Talking with God or to God) can feel as elusive as trying to grasp the wind, especially when distractions and uncertainties cloud your path. You're not alone in this quest for spiritual connection and understanding. Whether you're trying to integrate prayer into your life for the first time or aim to deepen your existing practice, questions about its significance and the obstacles faced are common. In this chapter, we'll uncover the core purpose of prayer, explore its dynamic benefits, and guide you towards practical routines that enhance **your communication with the divine** (The Loving Connection with our Celestial Father) through the power of prayer, while navigating any barriers that arise.

Purpose & Dynamics of *Prayer

*Prayer acts as a *personal dialogue with God, nurturing the divine relationship. It's akin to the way we maintain our earthly bonds through communication. We all know how essential it is to talk and spend time with loved ones. Similarly, prayer allows us to draw closer to God by opening our hearts to divine guidance and wisdom, expressing our thoughts and emotions candidly. As it says in James 4:8, drawing near to God invites Him to draw near to us as well. Moments of prayer can bring peace that surpasses understanding, as described by Hall, (2024). Whether dealing with grief or joy, prayer provides the opportunity to connect deeply and feel God's comforting presence.

This connection is more than just emotional support; it's a source of spiritual strength. When faced with life's obstacles, regular prayer fortifies our spiritual resilience. It's like having a lifeline, as illustrated when navigating the loss of a loved one. Prayer offers solace and acts as a recharge for the soul, giving believers a sense of peace and security. Its importance is well-documented. For instance, prayer can buffer stress, acting as a coping mechanism that promotes well-being by

reducing negative affect. (Newman et al., 2023).
In challenging times, the practice of prayer helps maintain hope and focus on what truly matters, allowing us to walk through difficulties without feeling overwhelmed. The Bible calls us to be anxious for nothing, and prayer enables us to align ourselves with this principle.

Aligning with God's will is another profound benefit of prayer. While we often navigate life with our desires and ambitions, prayer encourages us to reflect and see our goals from a divine perspective. This alignment is not just about giving up personal ambitions but finding **clarity and direction**. For **Jesus**, prayer was a means to align His will with the Father's, **offering a template** for meaningful communication with God. (Hall, 2024). Our prayers enable us to step back, self-reflect, and adjust our plans according to a higher purpose. Whether it's deciding on a career move or dealing with personal relationships, **prayer opens the door to wisdom and understanding beyond our knowledge.**

Furthermore, prayer fosters personal reflection and spiritual enlightenment. It's a platform for introspection, allowing us to assess our thoughts, actions, and motivations. Just like a mirror reflects our physical self, prayer can reflect our spiritual state, leading to deep insights about our lives. The quiet moments in prayer grant us the space to understand our spiritual journey. It's similar to having a conversation with a confidant, where we lay bare our fears and aspirations, finding clarity amidst chaos. This process of introspection doesn't just lead to self-awareness but often results in profound revelations about our path and purpose.

In today's world, where life is fast-paced and filled with constant noise, **prayer acts as a sanctuary.** It's a place where we can retreat and find the peace and clarity we seek. <u>Prayer is more than a routine</u>; it's an intentional practice of fostering a relationship with the divine. As we talk and spend time in prayer, our understanding deepens, allowing us **to connect more profoundly with our Father God**. It's this consistent dialogue that enriches every aspect of our spiritual life, providing guidance, support, and the strength to face whatever comes our way.

The next topic in this exploration is developing a structured approach to establishing a daily prayer habit. It's not enough to occasionally dip into prayer; a robust spiritual life thrives on consistency. A forthcoming section will delve into practical methods for building this habit, covering setting specific times, choosing conducive environments, and exploring varied prayer styles. Additionally, it will encourage tracking spiritual growth through journaling, ensuring a comprehensive understanding of prayer and its transformative power in our lives.

Developing a Consistent and Purposeful Prayer Practice

In the previous section, we explored the profound impact prayer has as a vital mode of spiritual connectivity and alignment with God's will. Building upon this understanding, we now delve into the practical frameworks for integrating prayer into everyday life to facilitate a consistent and enriching spiritual routine. Establishing a daily practice begins with understanding how the structured timing of prayer can become a cornerstone of spiritual strength and intentional living.

Studies have shown that when you set specific times for prayer, it promotes a rhythm of consistency and fosters a deeper sense of accountability. (Newman et al., 2023). For instance, an individual might decide to start the day with **morning prayers** and conclude it with an **evening session**. This habit not only brackets the day with moments of reflection and connection with the divine but also creates a heightened sense of awareness and anticipation for these times of reflection. Such scheduling nurtures discipline within spiritual practices and offers a robust framework where prayer transitions from an occasional act into an integral part of daily life.

Take John, for example, a busy father of three who initially struggled to find time for his spiritual needs. By consciously dedicating a separate time each evening, free from his familial obligations, John successfully integrated a prayer routine into his schedule. Not only did this decision enhance his spiritual connection, but it also provided him a sanctuary of peace at the end of hectic days, fostering stronger spiritual habits, (How, 2023). Such examples illustrate that while setting times might initially require adjustment, the long-term benefits significantly outweigh the initial efforts involved.

In conjunction with setting times, selecting an appropriate environment for prayer is equally pivotal. A quiet and comfortable space creates an atmosphere conducive to contemplation. A corner adorned with a deemed light lamp or a simple chair by the window can dramatically transform the prayer experience by promoting focus and minimizing distractions. Transformative changes occur when one personalizes these spaces; even the smallest shrine or altar in a busy home can become a sacred sanctuary where distractions fade, allowing deep personal encounters with our Father God. (Newman et al., 2023).

Consider Sarah, who transformed a small nook of her apartment into a dedicated prayer space with a cushion, an aromatic candle, and her favorite scriptures. She found the atmosphere so inviting and sacred that it became her go-to spot throughout the day, not only for prayer but for moments of quiet reflection and gratitude. In making prayer spaces personal, individuals often find an enhanced connection, as the environment supports their spiritual journey by offering a tangible reminder of their spiritual commitments (How, 2023).

Another essential aspect of sustaining engagement in prayer is embracing variety within practice. Different styles like meditation in the scriptures and through the scriptures, expressions of gratitude, and intercession for the needs of others, serve various emotional and spiritual needs. (Newman et al., 2023). Meditation in ad with the scriptures, for instance, can help center the mind and heart in God's word, while prayers of gratitude encourage reflection on daily blessings, which can foster a positive mindset. Intercessory prayer, focusing on the needs of others, broadens spiritual perspective and deepens empathy.

Rituals and practices can evolve to match these style shifts. Mike, who initially focused his prayers on supplication, found a new depth when incorporating gratitude, which transformed his perspective from one of need to thankfulness. This shift not only deepened his connection but also instilled a sense of ongoing engagement and fulfillment. (How, 2023). By varying prayer types, you can sustain a dynamic practice that adapts to changing moods and spiritual needs.

Journaling prayer experiences further enriches this journey by offering a tangible record of spiritual growth. Recording thoughts, reflections, and personal prayers in a journal allows for a unique form of reflection. This documentation creates an archive to revisit in times of doubt or during deep contemplation. As individuals read past entries, they gain insight into personal patterns, growth points, and areas needing focus. Moreover, seeing answered prayers can reaffirm faith and inspire gratitude, thereby reinforcing positive cycles of spiritual development. (Newman et al., 2023).

For instance, Lisa, an avid journaler, noted her prayers in a dedicated notebook. Over time, when reviewing previous entries, she discerned patterns in her thoughts and prayers, noticing how seemingly insurmountable obstacles had been overcome or transformed. This awareness not only provided immense encouragement but also pointed her toward personal growth areas, leading to a deeper understanding of her spiritual journey. (How, 2023).

To pray effectively, strategic prayer points help focus intention and enhance the impact of prayer. Identifying these focal areas allows individuals to target specific needs or themes, bringing clarity and purpose to their prayers. This method not only sharpens prayer effectiveness but also promotes accountability as individuals can reflect on their intentions and progress over time.

Consider a scenario where an individual struggling with doubt regularly prays for increased faith and clarity. By identifying faith as a strategic prayer point, they can focus their spiritual energy on this area, reinforcing it with consistent prayer and reflection. This focused approach can foster a stronger and more meaningful prayer experience, creating a bridge between intention and spiritual action. (Newman et al., 2023).

As we transition to the next section, it's important to note that while these strategies can make prayer routine more enriching, various barriers might hinder one's spiritual practice. The upcoming content will explore obstacles such as mundane routines, distractions, and doubts, offering methods to recognize and overcome these challenges. Through understanding and addressing these barriers, readers can further enrich their practice and find a deeper, more fulfilling prayer life.

Overcoming Barriers to Effective Prayer

Recognizing common barriers in prayer can turn these obstacles into opportunities for personal growth and enrich one's spiritual connection. Mundane routines can often lead to a stale prayer life. The repetitive nature of uninspired prayer practices can make spiritual communication feel like a task, stripping away the joy and warmth it once provided. Renewing enthusiasm is vital. Consider these strategies:

•   Change physical settings to refresh the experience. Praying outside, in a new room, or at different times of day can alter the ambiance.

•   Vary prayer styles and approaches. Introducing Adoration/worship prayers, practicing meditational in silence prayers, or playing instrumental praises contemplative music that can renew engagement.

•   Use visual reminders verses in a note card, a frame on the wall in your living room/office or any alert/remainder device at certain time of the day, as aids to create a constant and more immersive experience.

Simple adjustments can prevent prayer from turning into mere habit. For instance, incorporating gratitude each day can transform a rote list of requests into a dynamic spiritual practice.

Distractions are inevitable, especially in today's fast-paced environment. When they occur during prayer, distractions can shift the focus away from spiritual intentions, leaving one's prayer time feeling fragmented and interrupted. Addressing this challenge involves crafting solutions that minimize interference:

• Designate a distraction-free zone, perhaps by choosing a room with minimal noise or visual clutter.

• Set a specific time for prayer when interruptions are least likely, informing others of this sacred slot.

• Utilize mindfulness techniques to reclaim focus. Breathwork or briefly acknowledging distractions without judgment can enhance concentration.

A practical example is creating a routine where digital devices are silenced or placed in another room, fostering an environment that encourages mindful prayer.

Handling doubt and fear can be particularly challenging since these emotions often plant seeds of uncertainty. They may lead individuals to question their relationship with God, creating an emotional blockade that inhibits openhearted communication. Recognizing these feelings as natural parts of one's spiritual journey can be empowering. Confrontation might involve:

•   Sharing doubts with trusted friends or spiritual mentors who can offer support and different perspectives, and at the same time praying together.

•   Engaging in deeper **dialogues with God**, openly expressing fears and uncertainties within **prayers**.

•   Reflecting on past instances where faith overcame doubt, reinforcing confidence in God's plan.

A scenario depicting transformation includes someone who openly voices their fears in prayer and journal reflections. This can be transformative, ushering a shift from anxiety to a stronger sense of trust.

Staying consistent in prayer proves essential for nurturing a relationship with God, akin to any meaningful relationship requiring regular communication. Consistency ensures a steady line of spiritual nourishment and growth, yet it can be easy to neglect this amidst daily life pressures. Here are actionable steps to maintain steadfastness:

- Set daily reminders or alarms to establish a disciplined routine.

- Integrate prayer into existing daily rituals, like during a morning coffee or evening walk, to ensure it fits seamlessly into the day.

- Engage with a community of like-minded individuals who can offer encouragement and accountability.

Regular group meet-ups or online forums can provide this sense of community, proving invaluable in maintaining a committed practice. Narratives of those who thrive in their prayer life often highlight the positive influence of such support systems.

In blending routines, combating distractions, and countering doubts, individuals strengthen their spiritual foundations. For example, some find balance through early morning journaling sessions, integrating reflective practices that weave in prayer, contemplation, and gratitude. Others thrive by aligning their prayer times with nature walks, benefiting from the tranquility and perspective offered by the natural world.

The key lies in finding what resounds personally, transforming prayer from an obligation into a profound expression of one's faith and values. By setting this course, you extend beyond just praying—it becomes a lifestyle aligning intentions, actions, and spiritual aspirations.

Consistent prayer nurtures self-discipline and willpower, enabling you to confront life's challenges with a fortified spirit. The routine and steadfast approach to prayer spills over into other life areas, aiding in developing habits essential for personal and spiritual growth. This holistic transformation becomes evident, and as spiritual resilience grows, the capability to embrace life's complexities in a more meaningful, centered way follows naturally.

Strategies for recognizing and addressing prayer barriers are practical yet personal. Through small, intentional changes, you find new ways to connect, refresh routines, and enrich spiritual life. This compass guides us not only toward deeper faith but also toward lives infused with authentic purpose and serenity.

Challenges, (being there) as; distractions, doubts, or the monotony of routine, can be reframed as pathways to a deeper, more enriching prayer life. By implementing practical strategies, engaging with supportive communities, and embracing flexibility, the hurdles of prayer become milestones on a journey toward spiritual growth and fulfillment. Even amid setbacks and challenges, the endeavor fosters an ongoing, dynamic relationship with God, capable of weathering life's storms with grace. Regular engagement in this spiritual practice doesn't merely sustain—it amplifies, invigorates, and unifies one's spiritual and daily life, radiating outward into every interaction, decision, and experience.

Citing the importance of consistency and community, perspectives here draw from existing insights, providing readers concrete, actionable methods. The intention is simple yet profound: transform prayer life challenges into gateways for deeper faith and a harmonious connection to God. As we navigate through the world of distractions and routine, this process redefines our spiritual journey, helping you discover meaning in every step taken toward a prayerful life. This approach recognizes the complex tapestry of prayer, facilitating not only spiritual communication but enriching every facet of life backed by the strength of consistency and community. Through understanding these challenges and implementing effective strategies, the endeavor to deepen one's faith becomes tangible, achievable, and fulfilling.

José E. Espinoza

Summary and Reflections

Having delved into **the profound significance of prayer** in spiritual life, we now understand its multifaceted role as **a personal dialogue with God**, a source of spiritual strength, and a means for self-reflection and alignment with God's will. This chapter has illuminated how prayer nurtures **our divine connection**, offering solace, guidance, and inner peace amidst life's trials. Equipped with this understanding, we are poised to implement practical strategies for developing a consistent and purposeful prayer practice. By setting specific times, choosing conducive environments, embracing varied prayer styles, and documenting our experiences through journaling, we create a robust foundation for spiritual growth. As prayer becomes an integral part of our daily lives, it strengthens our relationship with God, helping us navigate challenges with hope and resilience. Now that we recognize the barriers and transformative power of prayer, we are ready to deepen our faith journey and enrich our spiritual lives, ensuring that this sacred communication becomes a vibrant, life-sustaining force.

NEW LIFE In 3 Priorities of TRIUMPH

Formula and *Guide

on *how to PRAY (to Connect verbally with Our Celestial Father)

To Experience Triumphant Results

"...*When You Pray, ..."

"This, then is *how you should pray:

*"Our Father in Heaven, *hallowed* (Adored, Praised & Honored) *Be Your Name,*

*Your *Kingdom Come, Your *Will Be Done,*

On Earth as it is in Heaven"...

- Matthew 6: 7-10

José E. Espinoza

Reference List

Developing A Meaningful Prayer Life. (2021). Fellowship Denver Church. https://www.fellowshipdenver.org/blog/2021/11/27/developing-a-meaningful-prayer-life

Hall, A. (2024). *The Importance of Prayer in Our Daily Lives and How It Can Benefit Us in Many Ways — Think Eternity with Matt Brown.* Think Eternity. https://thinke.org/blog/the-importance-of-prayer-in-our-daily-lives

How. (2023, July 30). *RENEW NORTHWEST.* RENEW NORTHWEST. https://www.renewnorthwest.com/faith-life/how-to-develop-and-maintain-a-habit-of-daily-prayer

Newman, D. B., Nezlek, J. B., & Thrash, T. M. (2023, January 9). *The dynamics of prayer in daily life and implications for well-being.* Journal of Personality and Social Psychology. https://doi.org/10.1037/pspp0000454

Overcoming Prayer Challenges: Finding Consistency and Overcoming Distractions | Our Blog | m-89114. (2024). M-89114. https://torrancechurch.org/our-blog/overcoming-prayer-challenges-finding-consistency-and-overcoming-distractions/

Chapter 3:

Understanding and Living The

KINGDOM Mindset

Understanding what it means to live with a Kingdom mindset, **starts at the very core of Christian faith:** The **Bible.** Regular scripture study not only introduces believers to **God's principles** but also serves as the **compass, guiding** their spiritual journey. Engaging deeply with **biblical texts** provides wisdom necessary for living out **Kingdom values** daily. For instance, **Matthew 6:33** advises, **"Seek first His kingdom** and **His righteousness,** and all these things will be given to you as well."** This directive isn't just a theoretical statement; it's a call to action that demands **prioritizing God's Kingdom** over everyday concerns. As Christians delve into other passages like **Micah 6:8,** which encourages acting justly and loving mercy, they discover comprehensive instructions to shape their behavior. (Francis & Francis, 2025).

Mind renewal flows naturally from scripture study. It's about **transforming thoughts** to align with Kingdom values anew. **Engaging in prayers** with a focus on seeking clarity in God's will strengthens this cognitive transformation. By spending dedicated **time in prayer**, believers practice mindfulness, recognizing areas in their thoughts that require change. Wise mentorship plays a pivotal role in this transformation—mentors can provide insight and guidance to help identify and refute negative thought patterns. Furthermore, consistently reflecting on life decisions supports ethical behavior. An individual might experience a mindset shift when choosing to volunteer regularly at a local shelter, realizing the profound impact of their actions not just on themselves but on others, echoing Kingdom ethics. (Francis & Francis, 2025; 25 Integrity Bible Verse | Ministry Brands, 2024).

Acknowledging the **priorities within God's Kingdom** is crucial for living accordingly. Prioritization of personal spiritual growth enables an individual <u>to become more attuned to God's mission</u>, leading to a deeper commitment. This growth is often spurred by a community <u>focused on Kingdom goals</u>, engaging in missions, or supporting fellow believers. **Galatians 5:13**, which urges serving one another humbly in love, illustrates the <u>Kingdom priority</u> of selfless service. Introspection is vital here—by evaluating personal goals and actions regularly, believers ensure they remain **aligned with these priorities**. Practical applications might include dedicating time each week for collaboration with your local church or community service, reflecting on how **these activities further the Kingdom and spiritual growth.** (Francis & Francis, 2025; 25 Integrity Bible Verse | Ministry Brands, 2024).

Lifestyle alignment is where intent meets daily practice. Commitment to living by Kingdom values must visibly permeate everyday decisions. For instance, mornings set the tone for a day aligned with Kingdom principles. **Starting with prayer** or devotionals positions individuals to face the day with a focus on God's calling. This practice equips them to make intentional choices, whether in their work ethic or in personal interactions, mirroring **Colossians 3:23**'s counsel to **work heartily as for the Lord**. Such consistency in choices inspires others to pursue a similar path. Lifestyle auditing helps, examining which habits truly support or detract from a **Kingdom-first mentality**. This could involve reassessing time spent on pursuits that do not contribute to spiritual growth and finding more ways to serve and love others as a **Kingdom ambassador**. (Francis & Francis, 2025; 25 Integrity Bible Verse | Ministry Brands, 2024).

Recognizing obstacles to living with a Kingdom focus is the natural segue to understanding what challenges arise. Worldly distractions often deter even the most **committed from maintaining a Kingdom-centric life**. Navigating these requires an awareness of potential pitfalls—like the constant barrage of information and tasks—and a commitment to refocus on what truly matters. Practically, this could mean setting boundaries around time spent on technology or consumerism to maintain a clear sightline toward Kingdom aspirations. Additionally, standing firm in counter-cultural values presents its own set of challenges, requiring strength and confidence in one's faith **to live out biblical principles** in environments that might not support them fully.

NEW LIFE   In 3 Priorities of TRIUMPH

Balancing personal ambitions with Kingdom aspirations further complicates matters. Many people find it difficult to distinguish between personal success and **accomplishments that genuinely serve God's Kingdom**. This differentiation often becomes clearer through self-evaluation and prayerful reflection, asking fundamental questions like: **"Does this ambition align with Jesus's teachings?"** Regular adjustments to personal objectives ensure they remain intertwined with broader Kingdom goals. It may involve re-evaluating career plans that focus solely on wealth accumulation, instead seeking roles where one can serve others, **echoing Kingdom principles** like generosity and stewardship.

Ultimately, **the journey to sustain a Kingdom mindset demands resilience**. Yet, regular introspection, intentional living, and robust prayer life provide the tools needed to endure against challenges, showcasing the transformative power of adhering to Kingdom values in daily life. As believers understand and embrace this redirection, they enter a holistic Christian journey—one fostering individual growth and **extending blessings both inwardly and beyond**. The consistent <u>alignment of thoughts and actions with Kingdom priorities</u> aptly equips them for whatever lies ahead, even as they anticipate further exploring challenges in **prioritizing <u>The Kingdom of God and His Justice</u>.** These principles serve as a strong foundation to help persevere, encouraging steadfastness in a world filled with opposing forces.

NEW LIFE   In 3 Priorities of TRIUMPH

Overcoming Challenges in Kingdom-Focused Living

Integrating **Kingdom priorities into daily life** sets a foundation for addressing distractions that derail us from our spiritual goals. In today's world, secular success and worldly priorities often overshadow Kingdom-focused living. We face constant distractions, whether it's the endless pursuit of career achievements or the allure of material possessions, and these seemingly appealing goals can subtly lead us astray from our spiritual path.

Understanding distractions starts with acknowledgment of the subtle allure of these secular priorities. The strong pull of societal success can take precedence over spiritual growth, shifting focus away from eternal values to temporal achievements. For example, the constant connectivity brought by technology can saturate our time, dragging us into an endless stream of media and notifications. Taking purposeful technology breaks serves as a constructive practice to reduce this external noise. By allocating time away from screens, individuals can create space for reflection and prioritize their spiritual health. Clearly **defining boundaries**

becomes essential here, as it helps protect the sacred time necessary for spiritual practices such as prayer, Adoration/worship, or meditation in God's word through the bible.

Maintaining **focus on the Kingdom** can be challenging amidst life's various hurdles, yet it remains crucial. Regular personal check-ins are beneficial for ensuring that one's actions align with Kingdom values rather than being influenced by external pressures. Setting simple reminders or utilizing visual cues can effectively redirect one's thoughts and actions back towards these spiritual priorities. Whether it's a sticky note with a meaningful scripture next to a bathroom mirror or an app that sends daily affirmations to focus on spiritual truths, these tools **create opportunities for continued realignment with Kingdom goals.**

Community support emerges as another powerful aid in maintaining focus. Interactions with a supportive community can foster accountability and provide encouragement. This communal approach reflects the principles of many successful faith-oriented communities that thrive by supporting each other's spiritual journeys. As described by Draper. (2021), when functioning well, these communities amplify each individual's capacity to live a Kingdom-focused life through shared beliefs and mutual encouragement.

Living a counter-cultural existence offers a rewarding yet challenging experience. Residing outside mainstream norms requires a firm foundation in one's beliefs. This solid foundation empowers believers to remain resilient when societal pressures intensify. For example, some faith communities successfully maintain their focus on spiritual truths amidst widespread social changes. Their experiences highlight the value of understanding and holding fast to one's beliefs as a means to inspire others through the distinctiveness of a Kingdom lifestyle. When steadfast, these communities can exemplify an attractive alternative, drawing others towards Kingdom values through their unique living testimony.

In this season of conscious prioritization, it's critical to consider life's true priorities. For some, like those described by Joe Hill, reassessing how relationships with God affect daily interactions underscores the central importance of these connections. Discerning where personal agendas might conflict with spiritual pursuits is key.

Through such reflection, believers can better integrate Kingdom ambitions into daily life.

The journey towards sustained <u>spiritual victory</u> involves continually <u>prioritizing the Kingdom</u>. Recognizing distractions and realigning focus sets the stage for persevering in faith. Our forthcoming discussion will concentrate on achieving sustained spiritual wins by navigating life's inherent challenges. Exploring the theme of turning difficulties into spiritual victories will be at the core of this progression. Celebrating Kingdom wins, regardless of how small, reaffirms our commitment to our faith journey and encourages ongoing spiritual growth.

By **remaining vigilant** to these broader insights, believers can actively initiate a change in perspective, leading to more fulfilling, Kingdom-centered lives. Recognizing the inherent challenges, committing to practical solutions, and embracing community support not only enhance personal spiritual growth but inspire broader community impact. As we move forward, **continually revisiting these principles** ensures **a life firmly rooted in the Kingdom of God**, prepared for any distraction that may arise along the path.

NEW LIFE In 3 Priorities of TRIUMPH

Achieving and Celebrating Sustained Spiritual Victory

Overcoming distractions and/or Temptations is essential in **maintaining focus on the Kingdom of God,** and it opens the door to a life embedded with spiritual success. Distractions and worldly pressures often lure us away from our Kingdom priorities, but identifying these obstacles is the first step in reinforcing our devotion. Acknowledging the influence of such diversions sets the stage for a long-term commitment to our spiritual journey. The journey, while challenging, is rewarding. By recognizing barriers, we carve a clearer path to living a life of faith.

One practical strategy for sustaining spiritual victory involves perseverance. Perseverance in faith can be likened to the steady nurturing of a plant. Just as a plant requires consistent water and sunlight to thrive, our spiritual lives demand continuous faith and effort. This isn't to say hurdles won't arise; they undoubtedly will, as emphasized by Rick. (2014), who writes about the importance of keeping faith even when God's plan isn't entirely clear. Navigating these hurdles requires resilience, an unwavering belief that the struggles we face are stepping stones toward greater spiritual maturity.

Concrete examples abound in everyday experiences. Consider work-related challenges where ethical decisions might conflict with worldly expectations. Maintaining integrity aligns with Kingdom values, leading to personal victories that transcend into spiritual growth. Another example is navigating relationships—choosing forgiveness over grudges mirrors the kind of love the Gospel encourages us to emulate. Holding onto Kingdom principles in such situations yields a deeper sense of spiritual fulfillment, providing peace and purpose that worldly pursuits may fail to offer.

Fostering spiritual growth through life's challenges involves adjusting perspectives and attitudes. It is not merely about coping with problems but recognizing them as opportunities for divine intervention. Church discussions often point toward Jesus as the epitome of handling life's tribulations. Emulating such qualities doesn't mean avoiding life's chaos, but rather embracing it with the confidence that God equips us for each moment. (40 Days of Prayer | Pastor Kirk, 2018).

NEW LIFE   In 3 Priorities of TRIUMPH

A commitment to growth also involves seeking God's voice earnestly. Pastor Kirk. (2018) reminds us that **sharing the Gospel is an act of sharing good news**—joyfully spreading the message of Jesus' love. This view invites believers to let their daily lives reflect this truth, creating a ripple effect that touches those around them. By choosing to live out the Gospel, we engage in a constant faith journey that demands intentionality. This journey is seldom about quantifiable milestones but about the progression toward becoming more Christ-like with each choice we make.

The **celebration of victories** is another strategy integral to maintaining focus on the Kingdom. Celebrations aren't only about grand, life-changing successes; they are just as crucial for small, everyday triumphs. Recognizing and thanking God for even the smallest wins fosters gratitude and joy, two qualities that keep Kingdom work grounded in reality. Achievements, when acknowledged in faith, provide a wellspring of motivation and purpose, ensuring that believers continue on the path set before them.

Successes are contextual. For instance, **overcoming the temptation** to engage in gossip at the workplace may seem minor, yet it's a reflection of <u>prioritizing Kingdom values</u>. Each decision to act righteously underpins our understanding of God's character and deepens our faith experience, pushing us further along the spiritual path. Victory also lies in the ability to withstand societal pressures that challenge our beliefs. When we choose to stand firm, even when inconvenient or unpopular, it not only strengthens personal faith but also acts as a testament to what living for God looks like.

Progression in faith is inherent in its practice. <u>By continuously integrating Kingdom priorities into daily routines</u>, faith becomes a lived experience. This living theology shapes our choices and ultimately influences those within our communities. By embedding the teachings of Jesus in everyday interactions, believers gain deeper insights into the nature of God's kingdom. This consistency in action ensures that spirituality becomes an unshakable part of identity, driving us closer to the divine purpose.

The power of divine friendships is stressed by Rick. (2014), who talks about the profound impact of Godly friendships in sustaining faith journeys. Friendly companionship that roots itself in mutual encouragement and accountability exponentially grows our spiritual capacity. Surrounding ourselves with a community that uplifts Kingdom values enhances resilience, as we journey together and share each other's burdens as well as victories.

In conclusion, **building a life around Kingdom priorities** demands a balance of perseverance, purposeful engagement, and joyful celebration. As believers, we aim to weave faith seamlessly into every facet of life. Recognizing obstacles and consistently choosing Kingdom ways turns us into vessels through which God can work mightily. By prioritizing the **Kingdom, victory** becomes a lifelong pursuit. This journey, while arduous at times, is graced with divine encounters and unforgettable moments of triumph, ensuring that our focus on God is sustained and our spiritual goals are fulfilled.

José E. Espinoza

Summary and Reflections

As we conclude our exploration of **prioritizing the Kingdom of God**, it's clear that adopting **a Kingdom mindset** isn't just essential—it transforms how we live daily. By focusing on scriptural wisdom, engaging deeply in **prayer**, and seeking guidance from mentors and community, we can cultivate a lifestyle aligned with God's principles. Though challenges like distractions and societal pressures may arise, recognizing these obstacles empowers us **to stay focused on what truly matters**. Now that we understand the importance of living with a Kingdom focus, we can take practical steps forward—embracing regular reflection, committing to spiritual growth, and celebrating even small victories as they lead us toward greater spiritual maturity. This journey is not one we undertake alone; it thrives best in the company of others who share our faith, offering encouragement and accountability. As we continue this path, let us strive **to weave Kingdom values** into every aspect of our lives, paving the way for **a life rich in purpose,** resilience, and **divine connection.**

NEW LIFE In 3 Priorities of TRIUMPH

Reference List

25 Integrity Bible Verse | Ministry Brands. (2024). Ministrybrands.com. https://www.ministrybrands.com/church-management/integrity-in-the-bible

40 Days of Prayer | Pastor Kirk. (2018). Pastor Kirk. https://pastorkirk.com/files/category-40-days-of-prayer.html

Draper, S. (2021, March 18). *Effervescence Accelerators: Barriers to Outsiders in Christian Interaction Rituals*. Sociology of Religion. https://doi.org/10.1093/socrel/srab001

Francis, I., & Francis, I. (2025, March 3). *How to Seek First the Kingdom of God: 7 Keys for Daily Life - Growing in Time*. Growing in Time -. https://growingintime.com/how-to-seek-first-the-kingdom-of-god/

Learning From Each Other: Obstacles Limiting Growth - Tidings. (2020, July 2). Tidings. https://tidings.org/articles/learning-from-each-other/

Rick. (2014, October 27). *God is a God of Progression*. Today's Word with Rick Pina; Today's Word with Rick Pina. http://todaysword.org/2014/10/27/god-god-progression/

José E. Espinoza

Part 2:

BIBLE

AUTHORITY: As The Word of God

Chapter 4:

Accepting the Authority of the Bible

Have you ever found yourself at a crossroads, unsure of which moral path to follow? Have you questioned where **to seek guidance** amidst life's perplexities? As Christians, navigating the journey of faith is often accompanied by these pressing inquiries. In an ever-changing world, understanding what anchors our beliefs can be a daunting task. **The Bible,** filled with ancient wisdom and divine teachings, presents itself as the word of God, as the **Decree of the King of kings,** And as the Maxima **Supreme Authority.**

In this chapter, we delve into how recognizing the Bible's ultimate authority profoundly influences a Christian's obedience and practical living. By embracing scripture as the foundation of faith, believers are invited to align their lives with **God's intentions,** transforming personal and communal aspects of existence. Through exploring the depth of **biblical authority,** we aim to reveal how it shapes decisions, fosters growth, and reinforces the acknowledgment of **God's sovereignty in our lives**.

Understanding Biblical Authority

The concept of biblical authority significantly influences the Christian journey, serving <u>as a guide for moral decisions</u>, community relationships, and the understanding of God's sovereignty. At the core lies the **Bible's supreme authority**, directing followers toward a life <u>aligned with divine intentions</u>. By exploring this foundational principle, we gain insight into the transformative power of scripture and how it shapes the Christian community, or (we can say) '<u>how these principles govern the people</u> of <u>The Kingdom of God here on Earth</u>.

Historically, the Bible's authority emerged through a tapestry of religious traditions and decisions made by early church councils. These historical contexts illuminate how believers formed a structured faith system that acknowledged scripture as <u>God's ultimate decree</u>.

Such acceptance empowered Christians to engage with the scripture logically and intellectually, **deciphering God's will** by <u>recognizing scripture as both</u> a <u>divine and human collaborative</u> creation. The 16th-century Protestant Reformation further cemented the Bible's centrality, spearheaded by reformers who challenged ecclesiastical authority, championing the scripture's supremacy over man-made traditions. (Franklin, 2018).

Central to this discussion is **sola Scriptura**, which insists that the Bible stands as the <u>ultimate authority for faith and practice</u>, requiring complete trust and adherence from believers. The reformers' steadfast commitment to this principle emboldened them to question established norms, advocating for a direct relationship with scriptures rather than intermediation by church authorities. As **Martin Luther** famously contended, true understanding of God stems directly from scripture, a belief underpinning his **challenge** to ecclesiastical conventions. (Franklin, 2018).

This historical legacy remains relevant, with modern Christians urged to delve into the scripture, critically discern its teachings, and integrate them into their daily lives. Scripture remains a chorus of timeless voices, inviting believers to listen actively and engage thoughtfully. This dialogical approach ensures scripture's authority manifests through continuous usage in teaching, preaching, and living out faith principles. (On Biblical Authority: A Dialogue, 2021).

Personal testimonies bear witness to the Bible's transformative energy. Individuals who embrace biblical authority often undergo life-changing shifts, seeing enhanced personal and communal relationships as a result. Obedience to biblical mandates fosters communities centered on service, outreach, and mutual support, reflecting God's kindness and mercy. It showcases how aligning life with biblical teachings leads to profound personal and communal growth.

Biblical authority influences moral decision-making, with scripture serving as the moral compass guiding complex choices and ethical dilemmas. When facing challenging decisions, Christians often reference scripture for insights and wisdom, relying on its timeless principles to navigate modern issues. This reliance underscores the **Bible as an authoritative guide** in a world rife with moral ambiguities, providing clarity and direction.

Moreover, **the Bible's authority** extends into shaping community dynamics. By embracing scriptural teachings, communities cultivate environments grounded in love, respect, and service. The church, as a collective body, leans on these principles to guide interactions within and outside their circles, striving to embody Christ's teachings. This adherence establishes a unique identity rooted in shared values and a commitment to living out biblical truths.

The diverse **voices within scripture** emphasize its authoritative nature, <u>revealing divine intentions across historical contexts</u>. The acknowledgment of God's character, as displayed in the scriptures, links God's benevolence and faithfulness with human understanding of compassion and mercy. This depiction encourages believers to embody these divine traits, fostering communities where kindness prevails and reflecting God's nature in human interactions. (On Biblical Authority: A Dialogue, 2021).

Challenges to biblical authority reflect ongoing debates surrounding its interpretation, especially when scrutinized through modern lenses. The authority's misuse throughout history, evidenced in instances of oppression and moral failings, compels believers to reconcile past transgressions with current values and ensure scriptures guide ethically righteous paths. By reflecting on such histories, Christians strive to uphold biblical truths without replicating historical wrongs, thus affirming scripture as a force for good.

Despite historical missteps, **the authority of the Bible remains an anchor** in turbulent waters, providing stability and reassurance. It equips believers with resilience in adversity, encouraging steadfast faith rooted in scripture. The Bible's guidance offers believers strength and solace, reaffirming their trust in divine promises.

As we move toward discussing **the active role of obedience in a new Christian life**, it becomes clear that daily practices solidify scriptural authority. Engaging in prayer, meditation, and scripture application nurtures spiritual growth, reinforcing faith's foundation and community bonds. This ongoing involvement aligns personal aspirations with divine intentions, encouraging believers to live thoughtfully and faithfully.

The transformative power of biblical authority reveals itself through active engagement with scripture, fostering communities characterized by harmony, moral clarity, and faithful devotion. In a world ripe with challenges, adhering to the Bible ensures believers remain steadfast and true to their spiritual calling, **heralding a future grounded in divine wisdom and grace**. We will now transition to discussing how daily practices form the bedrock of this newfound Christian life, highlighting the growth that emanates from consistent obedience to biblical teachings.

Living in Obedience

Recognizing the Bible's supreme authority sets the stage for an essential transition, moving from understanding its power to applying its teachings in daily life. While acknowledging the Bible's authority is foundational, living in obedience to its guidance takes commitment. This section explores how to practically live out biblical principles, especially for new Christians seeking to align their lives with these teachings.

Developing daily practices rooted in biblical teachings can deepen one's faith and encourage consistent obedience. Start by setting aside specific times each day for spiritual activities, such as prayer, meditation, journaling, and seeking accountability. Prayer and meditation serve as channels of communication and reflection, allowing you to engage with God's Word and discern His direction for your life. Journaling can be a powerful tool for documenting your spiritual journey, keeping track of insights, prayers, and personal growth. <u>Accountability</u>, whether through **a trusted friend or a spiritual mentor**, offers support in maintaining these practices and helps you stay on track.

Integrating scripture into decision-making requires intentional engagement. Begin by memorizing verses that resonate with your life circumstances or moral challenges. For example, if facing anxiety, recalling **Philippians 4:6-7** about being anxious for nothing anchors your thoughts in God's peace. Memorization empowers you to draw upon these scriptures in daily choices, reinforcing the importance of aligning decisions with biblical values. This approach influences not only personal decisions but also fosters community accountability, creating environments where shared scripture guides collective moral intuition and actions.

Mindful living, enriched by biblical principles, encourages intentionality and gratitude. Engaging the Bible regularly invites reflection on its teachings, providing clarity and direction in everyday actions. Mindfulness, coupled with scriptural reflection, transforms routine activities into opportunities for gratitude and awareness. This mental framework encourages acknowledging God's presence in every moment, deepening your spiritual life.

Community reflection plays a vital role in reinforcing obedience and promoting spiritual growth. Engaging in group discussions, shared **Bible study**, and collaborative actions strengthens individual faith and enhances communal understanding. For instance, participating in a **Bible study group** provides a platform for exploring diverse interpretations, sharing personal experiences, and expanding one's comprehension of God's Word. This collaborative environment also nurtures support systems where individuals encourage each other to live obediently by discussing struggles and celebrating spiritual victories.

Transitioning to the next section involves integrating biblical teachings into daily actions, translating the active obedience explored here into tangible strategies. For example, using biblical principles in goal-setting ensures that **ambitions**

align with God's will, fostering integrity and kindness. Observing the lives of role models who exemplify these teachings further inspires Christians to adopt similar practices.

Understanding and embracing the authority of the Bible guides believers through faith-centered living. Engaging comprehensively in daily practices, applying scripture, living mindfully, and participating in community discussions fuels growth. Each of these aspects combines to foster obedience, anchoring individuals in their faith as they journey through life. Through this active living, the transformative power of God's Word becomes evident, impacting personal and communal existence. Moreover, this discussion sets the groundwork for everyday integration of biblical teachings, as will be further explored in subsequent topics.

Practicality in Christian Living

Living out biblical teachings demands a shift from mere internal reflection to actionable behavior. This shift emphasizes the notion of "living in obedience," as discussed previously, showcasing how adherence to scripture can manifest in daily life. The core aim here is to embody a Christian lifestyle where beliefs seamlessly translate into everyday actions, adopting a cohesive faith experience where theory meets practice; as a living testimony (witnessing) The Kingdom of God among us.

Consider how setting specific goals can help individuals translate their faith into tangible actions. If one reads about the importance of stewardship in the Bible, setting a financial goal that includes tithing or supporting a charitable cause turns that teaching into a practical step. This not only aligns daily financial decisions with Christian values but also reinforces a mindset where every financial choice reflects a commitment to God's teachings. It's like living out the parable of the talents, where each decision to save, spend, or give becomes an act of faith.

Furthermore, embodying kindness extends beyond just a good deed; it reflects the essence of Christian teachings. By consciously deciding to show kindness to others, believers emulate stories like those of Ruth, who consistently demonstrated loyalty and compassion. Imagine helping a new neighbor settle into a community, offering meals or assistance moving in. These actions not only embody kindness but also create opportunities for building relationships grounded in Christian love and service.

Integrating reminders of biblical lessons into daily routines further deepens this connection between belief and practice. Engaging with scripture regularly, perhaps on a morning walk or during a coffee break, reinforces spiritual principles that guide daily actions. Individuals might recall Daniel's unwavering prayer life when faced with personal challenges, turning to meditation or prayer at specific times each day to seek guidance and strength. Such rituals, inspired by biblical characters, strengthen a spiritual foundation that directly influences choices and reactions throughout the day.

Real-life stories further highlight the successful integration of faith into everyday actions. Take Joe, who, in striving to emulate Christ's patience and forgiveness, chooses to navigate workplace conflicts with calmness and understanding. By consciously aligning his actions with biblical teachings, he not only resolves disputes with grace but also exemplifies a living testament to his faith. His approach fosters a peaceful work environment where his colleagues see a reflection of Christian values in practice, promoting respect and collaboration.

This translation of biblical teachings into tangible deeds creates an environment where ethical decisions become second nature. It's akin to working towards ethical behavior outlined in Source 1, promoting honesty and integrity. (University, 2024). Whether it's choosing transparency in business dealings or ensuring personal interactions are sincere, these decisions are grounded in a biblical framework that encourages moral living in all facets of life.

Considering character development in this context, biblical narratives provide a wealth of lessons applicable to modern life. By studying characters such as David, one finds inspiration for leadership marked by humility and resilience. Applying these lessons in a contemporary setting might involve leading a team at work with a servant's heart, prioritizing group success over personal gain. This leadership style, rooted in biblical teachings, nurtures an atmosphere of mutual respect and collaborative achievement.

The aim of fostering an environment where beliefs and actions align is not to promote rigid adherence, but to nurture an embodied faith that grows through lived experience. As Source 2 outlines, effective teaching strategies involve active engagement, prompting individuals to interpret and apply biblical principles. (Central Christian Academy, 2024). This principle applies equally to personal faith journeys, where engagement with scripture is lived out in real-world contexts, prompting transformation in thought and action.

Service opportunities further offer profound ways to embody faith. Organizing charity drives or community service projects in alignment with biblical teachings on compassion and service reflects an active commitment to faith in action. These projects provide not only direct aid to those in need but also cultivate a spirit of giving and communal responsibility. They serve as real-life applications of biblical principles, such as the command to "love your neighbor," highlighting how faith-driven actions uplift both giver and receiver.

Moreover, engaging the wider community through these actions strengthens communal bonds and showcases the transformative potential of Christian teachings. As one navigates the dynamics of family, work, and social interactions, these everyday applications of biblical lessons foster environments rich with empathy, support, and shared growth, mirroring the collaborative ethos described in Source 2's emphasis on community involvement. (Central Christian Academy, 2024).

As these principles weave into daily life, preparing for the next discussion on recognizing God's sovereignty becomes natural. This transition acknowledges that such practical applications are rooted in a deep understanding of biblical authority. It's this acknowledgment of God's sovereignty that ensures teachings are not just words, but living frameworks guiding everyday actions, as highlighted in the journey toward a Christ-centered worldview. (University, 2024).

In seamlessly integrating these aspects of faith into action, individuals construct a faith experience where belief and practice are indistinguishable. This approach nurtures a life where biblical teachings inspire real-world impact, preparing one not only to understand God's sovereignty but to live as a testament to His guiding presence.

NEW LIFE In 3 Priorities of TRIUMPH

The King of Kings: Source of Authority

As we delve into how biblical teachings turn into daily actions, it's essential to recognize that the Bible's authority underpins and guides Christian life. The profound authority vested in the Bible is rooted in **God's sovereignty**, a fundamental concept that significantly impacts Christianity's understanding of obedience and practical living.

God's sovereignty, as highlighted in many scriptural examples, serves as the foundation for the Bible's authority. In diverging from human notions of power that often focus on control and dominance, God's sovereignty embodies a divine will that is unbounded and all-encompassing. This means that nothing can impede the fulfillment of His purposes. Job's declaration, "I know that you can do all things, and that no purpose of yours can be thwarted". **(Job 42:2)** acts as a testimony to this unassailable supremacy. (Piper, 2019). Such trust in an unwavering divine plan fosters a form of comfort among believers, particularly as they navigate the inherent uncertainties of life. The assurance that **"the purpose of the Lord that will stand"**. **(Proverbs 19:21)** highlights how God's sovereign will ultimately surpasses any transient, humanly-devised plans. (Piper, 2019).

Comparing earthly and divine kingship offers further insight into this extraordinary concept of authority. If we look at historical contexts, earthly kingship often reflects elements of divine rule, albeit in a limited capacity. Throughout history, earthly kings exercised authority akin to a manager or ruler over a state, aiming to shape and command societal order. However, God's rule exceeds mere governance; it reaches the essence of creation, redemption, and renewal. Earth's sovereigns, no matter their might, pale in comparison to a divine authority that not only organizes but lovingly reshapes and redeems human hearts and lives. Isaiah states, "**My counsel shall stand**, and **I will accomplish** <u>**all my purpose**</u>," affirming the distinctive nature of divine power. (Piper, 2019).

Delving into such differences helps highlight how believers can align personal will with God's. The path of a Christian life encourages submission of personal desires to align more closely with spiritual callings and divine plans. This is not a form of suppression, but rather an awakening to true freedom through faith. Historical rulers may have attempted to impose their will, yet biblical teachings guide believers to willingly offer their desires to God, aligning them with His sovereign will. This requires a recognition of personal limitations and an understanding that ultimate strength comes from divine guidance. God is not merely organizing; He's transforming lives and destinies through love and grace, calling believers to submit with joy for eventual glorification seen in examples like Joseph's tale where what was intended for evil was ultimately used for good. (Genesis 50:20). (Piper, 2019).

Living under God's sovereignty doesn't only entail obedience but also allows authentic worship and service to flourish. Recognizing God's authority inspires believers to approach life and worship with humility and gratitude. Accepting divine will nurtures reliance on grace, fundamentally shifting the believer's focus from earthly concerns to a more profound, spiritual perspective. Authority in biblical context is not about fear-induced compliance; it's an invitation to be part of God's greater plan, as noted by Wright. (2018). **Romans 11:33** portrays **God's wisdom and judgment as being "unsearchable" and "inscrutable,"** pointing to a depth of divine knowledge that surpasses human comprehension and evokes a profound form of worship based on trust and reverence. (Piper, 2019).

Moreover, understanding God's authority challenges and redefines worldly views of control. Unlike secular authorities that often emphasize maintaining order or imposing regulations, the Bible describes divine authority as one that liberates. This liberation comes through redemption, setting individuals free to fulfill their God-given potential. By exercising authority through human agents and Scripture, God invites participants into an ongoing narrative of spiritual renewal, rather than restricting them with rigid dictates. **God, through Scripture and Christ**, models authority as something that is transformational and restorative, rather than coercive and limiting. In real terms, believers experience this through authentic expressions of faith in their communities, service to others, and living out scriptural imperatives not as mere rules but as liberating truths.

Ultimately, the reading and application of Scripture, as inspired by God's power and character, offer not mere answers to life's questions but rather a pathway to enter into a dynamic relationship with a sovereign Creator. The acknowledgment of God's ultimate authority bestows meaning, depth, and direction to Christian life, urging believers to pursue obedience out of a heartfelt desire to mirror divine love and justice. It prompts believers not only to see the Bible as an authoritative text but as a vehicle for God's love and purpose, reshaping hearts and communities.

The chapter vividly illustrates that the recognition of biblical authority deeply influences a Christian's every dimension of life. It is a call to integrate divine teachings into daily actions confidently, addressing uncertainties with the strength drawn from faith in a sovereign God. Through this lens, God's sovereignty becomes a source of profound assurance and joy, empowering believers to surrender personal ambitions and fears in favor of divine wisdom and purpose. This forms the bedrock of a vibrant faith where gratitude, humility, and spiritual growth become intricately woven into the fabric of everyday life.

Summary and Reflections

Now that we recognize the Bible as the ultimate authority in a Christian's life, we can begin to see how this deep acknowledgment transforms both individuals and communities. It guides our decisions, nurtures our relationships, and reaffirms God's sovereignty in every aspect of our existence. As we embrace scripture's teachings, we are empowered to live obediently, aligning our actions with divine principles. This creates a ripple effect, fostering environments characterized by love, respect, and service. By actively engaging with biblical truths, we not only deepen our faith but also inspire others to explore the depths of God's wisdom and grace. This commitment sets the foundation for a vibrant spiritual journey where God's purposes guide us, enlightening our paths and ensuring that we live out our faith with joy and purpose.

NEW LIFE In 3 Priorities of TRIUMPH

Reference List

Central Christian Academy. (2024, June 12). *Integrating Biblical Studies: A Guide for Curriculum Development | Central Christian Academy.* Central Christian Academy. https://ccachargers.org/blog/2024/06/12/integrating-biblical-studies-for-curriculum-development/

Franklin, K. J. (2018, February 14). *How can the Reformation's focus on faithfulness to Scripture inspire us for mission?*HTS Teologiese Studies / Theological Studies. https://doi.org/10.4102/hts.v74i1.4817

On Biblical Authority: A Dialogue. (2021). Ministrymatters.com. https://www.ministrymatters.com/preach/entry/10847/on-biblical-authority-a-dialogue

PRACTICAL TIPS AND GUIDANCE FOR SPIRITUAL GROWTH AND DISCIPLESHIP. (2024). Grace Church Plano. https://graceplano.church/blog/2024/09/18/practical-tips-and-guidance-for-spiritual-growth-and-discipleship

Piper, J. (2019, April 8). *What Is the Sovereignty of God?* Www.desiringgod.org. https://www.desiringgod.org/interviews/what-is-the-sovereignty-of-god

University, C. C. (2024). *Teaching With a Biblical Worldview | CCU Online.* Ccu.edu. https://www.ccu.edu/blogs/cags/category/education/teaching-with-a-biblical-worldview/

Wright, N. T. (2018, October 3). *N.T. Wright on Scripture and the Authority of God - Articles.* BioLogos. https://biologos.org/articles/n-t-wright-on-scripture-and-the-authority-of-god

mariannedavis0. (2024, May 31). *Bible Engagement: A Key to Spiritual Growth.* CBE. https://www.centerforbibleengagement.org/post/bible-engagement-a-key-to-spiritual-growth

José E. Espinoza

Chapter 5:

Biblical <u>Blessings</u> and <u>Promises</u>; Unveiled

In the midst of life's uncertainties, many individuals find themselves searching for anchors to hold onto. The quest for assurance in a world filled with unpredictable moments is familiar to countless believers and seekers alike. Such quests often lead some to look towards promises—those vital assurances that someone has their back, guiding them through even the stormiest of times. Yet, doubts persist. Do these promises truly offer the stability we yearn for, or are they merely comforting words devoid of power?

Within the pages of this chapter, we journey into the exploration of biblical blessings and promises, uncovering their profound significance in the Christian faith. By venturing into the heart of scripture, we will illuminate how divine promises not only guide us through challenges but also shape a life of purpose and resilience. These timeless assurances reveal a path to living victoriously under God's sovereignty, empowering believers to honor Him in every aspect of life while embracing eternal hope.

Understanding Divine Promises & Living a Victorious Life

Promises within the Bible form a bedrock for Christians, shaping a robust trust in God's character. Scripture highlights various promises spanning guidance, protection, and provision that cultivate faith. For example, God's promise to Abraham established a lineage that would inherit the earth, foregrounding His faithfulness despite life's uncertainties. These scriptural assurances help Christians weather life's storms by reinforcing God's unwavering commitment to their well-being. (What Does the Bible Say About Resilience?, n.d.).

Covenantal relationships reveal God's nature and His plans. Historical accounts, such as the Exodus covenant with Moses, illustrate how divine agreements structure the spiritual journey of believers, guiding them through their own wilderness experiences. By studying these covenants, Christians gain insight into how God interacts with His people and can find reassurance in His promises' timelessness. This understanding encourages spiritual growth. (What Does the Bible Say About Resilience?, n.d.).

In today's world, discerning biblical promises helps navigate modern challenges. By personalizing scriptural promises, believers find comfort. For instance, the promise of peace amid turmoil offers solace and direction during life's unpredictability. Embracing these promises not only provides hope but fortifies one's faith. Strategies such as meditative prayer or reflective journaling can make these promises a personal refuge in times of need. (**Ephesians 6: 10-18**, Resilient Faith / Spiritual Resilience, 2011).

The manifestation of promises arises when believers act in faith. Through prayer, community engagement, and personal testimonies, God's promises come alive. Collective prayer rallies and testimonies of divine intervention exemplify how faith in action deepens the evidence of these promises, reinforcing the belief in their power.

NEW LIFE   In 3 Priorities of TRIUMPH

This tangible realization emboldens believers, showcasing how promises provide a reliable foundation for life's trials. (Ephesians 6: 10-18, Resilient Faith / Spiritual Resilience, 2011).

Faith stands as the cornerstone of a victorious life. Trust in God's plan brings about an inner confidence, enabling one to face life's challenges with resilience. Stories of biblical figures like Joseph demonstrate the strength drawn from unshakeable faith. His ability to rise from slavery to a position of influence underscores how faith can turn adversity into triumph. This exemplifies how faith doesn't eradicate challenges but transforms one's approach to them. (What Does the Bible Say About Resilience?, n.d.).

Scripture provides wisdom during trials, offering encouragement through narratives of overcoming adversity. For example, David's resilience against Goliath illustrates how trust in God's promises can unlock unforeseen solutions. Biblical truths act as a lens to shift perspectives on hardships, unveiling new paths previously obscured by doubt. These narratives serve as a resource bank of inspiration, shining a light on the potential hidden in every struggle. (What Does the Bible Say About Resilience?, n.d.).

José E. Espinoza

Joy, a divine gift, underscores a victorious life, fostering a positive outlook that is contagious. Joy fuels perseverance, lifting the spirit beyond immediate circumstances. It serves as a reminder of God's everlasting presence and goodness, encouraging gratitude and a hopeful perspective on life. Joyful living spreads seeds of hope within communities, inspiring others to embrace divine promises as well. This transformative joy becomes an authentic reflection of faith in action. (**Ephesians 6: 10-18**, Resilient Faith / Spiritual Resilience, 2011).

Service provides a practical way to experience God's promises. Actively serving others reveals divine love and faithfulness, often in unexpected ways. Community service projects, such as feeding the homeless or mentoring youth, illustrate how collective efforts can manifest divine promises in the tangible world. In serving others, believers find themselves transforming communities and deepening their relationship with God. This mutual exchange of blessings highlights the essence of divine promises—God's intention for His love to spread through us. (What Does the Bible Say About Resilience?, n.d.).

NEW LIFE   In 3 Priorities of TRIUMPH

Transitioning to the next section involves contemplating how one receives blessings through faith, emphasizing gratitude, generosity, and witnessing as means to honor God daily. Gratitude practices cultivate an awareness of these blessings, nurturing a heart ready to give back. Generosity as worship reflects a commitment to share God's abundance with others, turning everyday acts into meaningful expressions of faith. Living as witnesses in our communities reveals the glory of God, integrating thanksgiving into our lives as a testament to His promises fulfilled.

Honoring God Through Blessings

Previously, we explored how divine promises in a Christian's life chart a biblical path to a victorious life through God's blessings. This section dives deeper into the practical side, showing how these blessings empower believers to honor and glorify God. It focuses on using blessings actively to enhance one's spiritual journey. Understanding their power is the first step; utilizing them provides a tangible way to worship and witness God's work in everyday life. Let's delve into how gratitude, generosity, and testimonies can embody this.

Gratitude isn't just thanking God during good times. It's about cultivating a grateful heart amidst every blessing, which fosters a humble and positive attitude. When you acknowledge God's gifts, you not only honor Him but also reshape your outlook from one of scarcity to abundance. Research indicates that expressing gratitude provides numerous psychological benefits, shifting focus from fear to joy (Omondi, 2023). Imagine a day where you consciously recognize every small blessing—be it the warmth of sunlight or a friend's smile—and you thank God for it. This simple practice can inspire others to do the same, creating a ripple effect among those around you. By sharing your gratitude, you encourage others to see their lives in a new light, effectively spreading positivity.

Generosity is another powerful way to worship God beyond mere rituals or obligatory acts. When you give, you're reflecting God's nature, as the ultimate giver himself. Acts of generosity, like volunteering time at a shelter or donating to a cause, strengthen community bonds and provide support to those in need. They transcend obligation, becoming joyful expressions of faith. For example, consider a time you saw someone in need and felt compelled to help not out of duty but pure love. This reflects the transformative power of giving, aligning with God's work on Earth. (View, 2020). Through generosity, you don't just give material support; you offer hope, showing others the loving nature of God's kingdom.

Testimonies hold power in honoring God's work by sharing personal stories of divine intervention and faithfulness. These narratives invite others into your experience, serving as reminders of the extraordinary in the ordinary. Imagine telling someone how a prayer was answered, or a challenge was overcome through faith. Personal stories make the intangible qualities of God's work real to others, strengthening community bonds. Sharing how you've seen God act not only honors Him but inspires others to reflect on their own journeys. It's a form of encouragement, showing that trials can lead to triumphs and obstacles can lead to deeper faith.

Living as witnesses means showcasing how you embody God's blessings in a way that inspires others. Authenticity in your actions fosters genuine discussions about faith. For instance, through kind words, active listening, or a simple act of kindness, you provide a living testament of God's love and work. **People often need real-life examples** to kickstart their own faith journey. When they see someone living out their beliefs authentically, it becomes a catalyst for change. Think of a situation where you exemplified forgiveness or patience, and how these actions can lead others to ponder their own journey. It's in these everyday actions that the true essence of a believer's life shines.

As we transition to the next section, we'll explore "Eternal Promises and Their Impact." This will delve into the eternal perspective of divine promises and heavenly assurance, influencing both current life decisions and the broader spectrum of existence. Understanding the eternal nature of divine promises gives depth to the blessings-focused approach we just discussed, adding layers of hope and assurance. Such promises offer a bigger picture view, guiding life with the reassurance of God's unending love and eternity. This transition builds on the foundation laid, showing how each blessing and act of witness is an integral part of the greater story God writes with our lives.

NEW LIFE   In 3 Priorities of TRIUMPH

This section seeks to equip believers with practical tools to navigate their spiritual path effectively. Recognizing how each aspect—gratitude, generosity, and testimony—acts as a steppingstone in realizing their full potential of honoring God is crucial. In this dynamic interaction between receiving and giving blessings, believers find true purpose. By embodying these principles, they act as living testaments to God's work, influencing their communities and beyond. The journey might be personal, but its impact is collective, shaping a community that thrives on mutual support and shared faith. As we continue exploring, remember the connections between promises, blessings, and their eternal impact on a believer's journey.

Eternal Promises and Their Impact

Gratitude and generosity unlock a deeper understanding of God's eternal promises, reflecting His work in our lives. Many believers consider these divine promises as anchors, particularly the promise of eternal life. This assurance offers hope and transforms every aspect of a believer's life.

José E. Espinoza

The promise of eternal life, like a beacon, inspires believers to live with intention and purpose. It's not merely about life after death but infuses meaning into our present lives. John 3:16's eternal invitation urges us to view our earthly journey as part of a broader spiritual narrative. (O Favored One, 2025). This understanding shapes decision-making, as believers align daily actions with this divine promise, seeking to honor God's plan and purpose along the way.

Leaving a legacy of faith becomes achievable when inspired by eternal promises. Just as biblical figures such as Joseph and Paul embraced God's future grace, they left spiritual legacies that echo through generations. (O Favored One, 2025). Their stories motivate believers to build their own legacies, grounded in faith and hope. When shared with younger generations, these legacies become spiritual inheritances, carrying forward principles and teachings rooted in divine promise.

Hope derived from eternal promises acts as an unwavering anchor. When life's challenges overwhelm, the promise of eternal grace reassures us of divine stability. This hope, rooted in the certainty of God's promises, enables believers to withstand life's storms without being swept away.

NEW LIFE   In 3 Priorities of TRIUMPH

(O Favored One, 2025). Christian hope transcends mere optimism; it is a profound trust in promises yet unseen and a confidence that strengthens in times of trouble.

The promise of a new heaven and earth in Revelation provides an incredible vision of divine restoration. John's revelation of a world free of sorrow, pain, and sin is a glimpse into God's promise of eternal utopia. Such a transformational promise compels us to lead lives marked by optimism and anticipation. (Osama Hamim, 2024). This vision encourages believers to view earthly trials with a lens focused on divine renewal and the bigger picture of God's redeeming work.

In grasping God's promise of eternal life, decision-making transforms, leaving believers contemplating choices that resonate with their faith. Recognizing promises strengthens faith and trust in God, encouraging decisions that transcend self-interest. Seeing biblical promises fulfilled, believers strive to align decisions in accordance, ensuring choices reflect a deeper understanding of God's ultimate plan.

The promise of redemption through Christ, often illustrated as Jesus being both the Alpha and Omega, signifies that He encompasses beginning and end, creation and salvation. (Osama Hamim, 2024). This acknowledgment urges believers to live intentionally, knowing that life's ultimate purpose is intertwined with Christ's eternal sovereignty. This perspective instills a sense of accountability, ensuring earthly actions mirror eternal implications.

Fulfilling promises in biblical narratives, like Joseph's rise from slavery to leadership, inspire modern believers. These stories demonstrate how trials, when viewed through the lens of divine promise, can lead to unforeseen grace and transformation. Joseph's unwavering faith, despite trials, exemplifies trust in God's unfaltering promises, showcasing how present struggles shall never define ultimate destinies. (O Favored One, 2025).

Spiritual disciplines, cultivated with future promise in mind, become vital for growth. Prayer, reflection, and scripture reading align believers with divine purpose, shifting focus to eternal significance rather than transient triumphs. **Colossians 2:7** emphasizes having roots in Him, forming a foundation that withstands time and trials. (O Favored One, 2025). Establishing such habits reinforces trust, fostering a resilient faith amid life's uncertainties.

Fulfilled promises in the Bible, chronicled as narratives of faith, hope, and trust, serve as monumental reminders to modern believers. Despite obstacles, the opportunity for divine assistance remains steadfast. Recognizing this throughout scriptures, believers cultivate a future-oriented faith achieved through proactive engagement with spiritual disciplines and reflection. (Osama Hamim, 2024).

Active faith practices sustain hope and mold a lifestyle centered around God's unfailing promises. Thoughtfully engaging with scripture and faith communities solidifies spiritual trust, ensuring a future gracefully envisioned and diligently embraced. (O Favored One, 2025). A believer's lifestyle, inherently reflective of eternal hope, becomes a testament to God's divine plan.

Faith communities play an essential role in nurturing this forward-looking faith. Through collective worship and shared experiences, believers find comfort and encouragement. This communal aspect, often a profound source of strength, reinforces the notion of shared eternal promises and mutual edification. Collective journeying ensures believers remain steadfast in life's trials, firmly anchored in eternal hope.

Engaging with promises, both personal and communal, reveals the myriad ways divine assurance transforms daily existence, encouraging actions aligned with eternal truths. As believers commit to understanding these promises' implications, they create space for spiritual growth and deeper engagement with God's unending grace.

Believers see life's trials as opportunities for growth when interpreting them through the lens of future grace. Faith practices centered around this perspective dissolve feelings of helplessness, replacing them with enduring hope. Encouraged by scriptural narratives of promise fulfillment, believers draw upon these lessons for guidance through contemporary challenges.

Ultimately, eternal promises offer a transformative impact on every facet of a believer's life. Aspiring to live in harmony with these promises, believers find peace amid chaos, strength amid tribulations, and purpose amid the mundane. Their lives reflect a dedication to embracing grace, continually seeking to honor God through gratitude, thus paving a path for future inheritors of faith. Such intentional living not only fulfills personal spiritual aspirations but contributes to an enduring community rooted in trust toward God's eternal covenant.

Summary and Reflections

As we conclude this chapter on divine promises and blessings, we've gained essential insights into how these biblical assurances guide us toward a victorious life that honors God's sovereignty. By understanding and embracing these promises, we discover their transformative power, enabling us to live with confidence in God's unwavering commitment to our wellbeing. With gratitude and generosity as acts of worship, our lives become testimonies of faith, impacting others positively. Together, let's actively apply these principles, ensuring our daily actions reflect our trust in God's eternal plan. Moving forward, may we continue nurturing our understanding and acceptance of divine promises, allowing them to influence our journey in faith, strengthening our communities, and embodying God's love in all we do.

NEW LIFE   In 3 Priorities of TRIUMPH

Reference List

Ephesians 6: 10-18, Resilient Faith / Spiritual Resilience. (2011, February 1). Brewster Baptist Church. https://brewsterbaptistchurch.org/resilient-faith-spiritual-resilience/

Omondi, B. (2023, September 15). *Learn How to Cultivate Gratitude Biblically - Bernard Omondi - Medium.* Medium. https://medium.com/@bernardomondi2020/learn-how-to-cultivate-a-spirit-of-gratitude-biblically-c78de6ae9129

O Favored One. (2025, February 4). *Future Grace: Finding Hope in God's Faithful Promises.* Humanities Site. https://ofavoredone.com/future-grace/

Osama Hamim. (2024, October 31). *The Promise of New Heaven and Earth: A Revelation of Eternal Hope.* Greg Lancaster Ministries. https://greglancaster.org/2024/10/the-promise-of-new-heaven-and-earth-a-revelation-of-eternal-hope.html

View. (2020, November 22). *The Power of Gratitude.* People Need Jesus; People Need Jesus. https://peopleneedjesus.net/2020/11/22/the-power-of-gratitude/

What Does the Bible Say About Resilience? (n.d.). Get.tithe.ly. https://get.tithe.ly/blog/what-does-the-bible-say-about-resilience

José E. Espinoza

Chapter 6:

Clarifying <u>Biblically</u> God's <u>Will</u>, <u>Justice</u>, and Love

Have you ever wondered how to truly understand someone's intentions and desires, especially when they seem intangible or mysterious? Imagine a world where you can not only glimpse another's heart but also align your life with their profound and purposeful plans. For many believers, comprehending God's will feels like navigating an enigma—yearning for divine guidance yet grappling with the everyday noise of life. How do we distinguish His voice from our own thoughts, and how can we comprehend the vast expanse of His love and justice?

In this chapter, we'll dive into these questions and more, offering insights on delving deeper into God's desires through scripture, acknowledging

NEW LIFE   In 3 Priorities of TRIUMPH

His loving promises, and discerning His justice as depicted in the Bible. We'll explore practical ways to integrate these spiritual truths into our lives, enabling us to reflect divine principles daily. Whether you're seeking direction, yearning for a more profound connection, or striving to live a life aligned with biblical teachings, this exploration of God's will, love, and justice will guide you on the path to greatness within the Kingdom of Heaven here on Earth.

Understanding God's Will and Love through the Bible

Deciphering God's will through the Bible involves developing habits of consistent reading and prayer, offering a path to divine guidance and insights. Biblical teachings suggest that God's message isn't revealed through sudden epiphanies but through a steady relationship with His Word. This daily commitment allows us to align our personal intentions with God's purposes, as we continuously open ourselves to divine communication. Through this practice, we become receptive to God's voice guiding us in our decisions.

Reading the Bible purposefully involves more than just understanding the text; it's about engaging with it actively. As you approach these scriptures, focusing intentionally on sections that deal with discernment and guidance can be especially enlightening. Consider **Proverbs 3:5-6**, ***"Trust in the Lord with all your heart and lean not on your own understanding."*** This encourages a shift from self-reliance to seeking spiritual wisdom. As you read, build reflection time into each session. Ask yourself: How does this apply to my current life choices? What might God be trying to tell me through these words? Such queries enable scripture to illuminate your path, providing clarity even amidst the complexity of daily life. (Institute, 2018).

Practicing prayer that incorporates scripture can deepen this dialogue with God. Using verses in prayer fosters a reciprocal conversation, anchoring our words in divine promises. Instead of merely asking for specific outcomes, we can **ask that our desires align with God's will**. For example, incorporating the language of **Psalm 25:8-9** into prayer can become a way to request guidance with a humble heart, asking God to lead us in His ways of truth and love. (Institute, 2018).

NEW LIFE   In 3 Priorities of TRIUMPH

Creating a peaceful environment for Bible study is crucial in enhancing one's ability to discern God's guidance. Begin by selecting an area free from distractions. Opt for a location where you can sit comfortably, access your Bible and any other materials, and won't be easily disrupted. Commence each Bible study session with a calming routine, such as lighting a candle or playing soft, meditative music, which helps your mind transition from the noise of the day to the focus of spiritual study.

Upon settling into your space, read the scripture aloud, allowing the sound to penetrate your awareness. This practice helps internalize the message, and speaking the words can often bring new understanding. After reading, take moments of stillness and reflection. Meditate on the passages, considering their personal implications. A pause after reading can allow the Holy Spirit to highlight particular phrases or lessons relevant to your current life situation.

As you make this part of your practice, pay attention to feelings or thoughts that resonate with biblical themes and align with God's will. This sensitivity helps you discern between internal voices and divine nudges. The Bible often reveals the character of God, showing His justice and love as guiding principles. Consider how you might emulate these qualities in your interactions and decisions.

A practical approach involves incorporating specific biblical exercises or journaling activities. Start each day or week by selecting a theme, such as guidance, love, or justice, and explore passages related to it throughout your study sessions. Write about how these passages speak to your current experiences, documenting insights and questions that arise.

To further this practice, engage in regular prayer that uses scriptural language. Draw upon verses like John 15:4-5, which emphasizes the importance of remaining in God as the source of our strength and purpose. Acknowledge that without this connection, attempts to bear fruit could falter, and invite God to help you abide in Him in every aspect of your life. (Charles, 2021).

Set aside time for continuous reevaluation of how your choices and actions align with scriptural teachings. Reflecting regularly can help underscore God's intentions and ensure your understanding deepens over time. Ask yourself questions like: Am I aligning my desires with

NEW LIFE   In 3 Priorities of TRIUMPH

God's? Are my actions reflective of the justice and love exemplified in scripture? This self-examination assists you in remaining attentive and responsive to God's leading.

This ongoing study and prayer initiative can transform your understanding and intimacy with God, clarifying His will through deepened familiarity with His Word. As you pursue this path, you may begin to notice patterns or themes reflecting God's desires for you. By faithfully engaging with scripture, you cultivate a relationship characterized by mutual exchange— your seeking met with God's guiding.

Promote spiritual growth by establishing these practices as a habit. Integrate them into your daily routine, ensuring they become a regular part of how you start or end your day. A quieter mind and spirit, coupled with thoughtful engagement, can help foster an environment where you can hear God's voice more clearly.

In the subsequent section, the focus will shift toward translating this understanding into action, exploring how divine love can manifest in everyday life, reinforcing the foundational knowledge of God's will, justice, and love established here. These practices of purposeful

Bible reading and prayer form the bedrock of recognizing divine guidance, offering you a blueprint for aligning your life more closely with God's intentions.

Justice and Community in the Kingdom of God

In the previous discussion, we identified how divine justice differs from human justice systems, particularly emphasizing **mercy**, grace, and **accountability**. Now it's crucial to explore how recognizing **God's justice** can inform our everyday lives. God's justice calls us to fairness, integrity, and accountability in our interactions with others. It's about aligning our lives with **divine principles, helping us to live justly**.

In practical terms, living justly means upholding fairness in our daily decisions. Many workplaces today emphasize ethical decision-making, echoing biblical principles. For instance, when we're in roles that require making decisions affecting others—such as hiring or resource allocation—the call to justice asks us to evaluate each person or situation on merit and need rather than personal bias. It means treating colleagues and employees with respect, offering equal opportunities for growth and advancement.

In sum, living justly isn't a passive affair. It's an active pursuit requiring us to weave biblical principles into each aspect of our lives. The thread of justice runs through actions of fairness at work, participation in community justice, and advocacy for marginalized groups, illustrating how divine teachings inform and transform our society. Implementing these ideas, we progressively embody **values resonating with God's kingdom**—values of love, humility, and generosity.

This exploration of justice as a foundational life principle naturally leads us to the next section on embodying the values of God's kingdom more broadly. When we practice justice, we lay a solid groundwork for a life characterized by deep love and humility, core values that drive a kingdom-focused existence. As we continue, we'll delve deeper into how these values can manifest, enabling us to live as reflections of divine light and justice in the world.

José E. Espinoza

Embodying Kingdom Values on Earth

Understanding divine justice offers a fresh perspective on life's complexities by showing how love and mercy can guide ethical living and community building. The idea that justice is not merely about fairness but involves love and mercy establishes a framework for how we should engage with others. This approach invites us to not only seek justice but to embody it in our everyday actions, creating a profound ripple effect within our communities. We transition now to the exploration of living out biblical values in our daily lives, inspired by this holistic view of justice.

At the heart of biblical living lies the integration of kingdom values into our character. Kingdom values, such as love, humility, and generosity, should become second nature, influencing our interactions and decisions. For example, generosity goes beyond financial giving—it extends to the time and energy we invest in others. By prioritizing acts of kindness and support, we visibly demonstrate what it means to live according to kingdom principles. The call is to infuse these values into the core of who we are, so they naturally manifest in our behaviors.

NEW LIFE   In 3 Priorities of TRIUMPH

Living in alignment with kingdom values can seem daunting, but practical steps simplify the process. The cultivation of a prayerful life is a foundational practice. Regular prayer equips us with divine insight and strength to navigate life's hurdles. Integrating scripture into daily routines offers guidance; scriptures remind us who we are and what we stand for, providing a roadmap for decision-making. Choosing to act in ways that are consistent with God's teachings ensures our lives reflect these scriptural truths. An eternal perspective keeps us rooted, guiding us to prioritize what truly matters in light of eternity rather than the transient nature of the world around us.

Building relationships based on eternal values transforms how we interact with others. Relationships grounded in love and humility flourish, offering a safe space for growth and learning. We're reminded of this in the idea of legacy—what we build during our time on Earth. Creating enduring connections based on shared values cements our impact, ensuring it extends long after we're gone. These relationships act as a testament to our faith and allow our principles to live on through the lives we've touched.

José E. Espinoza

Practical examples highlight the success of applying kingdom values in everyday life. Consider a community where residents make a concerted effort to live out these values. Their neighborhood thrives because their actions foster a supportive environment. They prioritize communal well-being over individual gain, which cultivates a diverse and welcoming community. Such examples illustrate that living by biblical values is achievable and that it yields rewarding outcomes.

Conversely, kingdom living is not without its challenges. Life frequently throws obstacles our way, testing our commitment to these values. However, it's in these times of adversity that our character and faith are strengthened. By continually aligning our responses with biblical principles, we not only grow as individuals but also inspire those around us. Setting an example in moments of difficulty reinforces the transformative power of living by kingdom values.

Another crucial aspect is the rejection of a scarcity mentality. God promises abundance, yet we often operate under the assumption that resources are limited. Recognizing God as our provider fosters a mindset of abundance, freeing us to give generously without fear. This approach to resources extends beyond money; it includes our talents and skills, which we can share freely to uplift others and fulfill our unique roles in building God's kingdom on Earth. (Mast & Mast, 2019).

Living as God's people demands intentionality in our actions and choices. We aspire to become more Christ-like by embodying His virtues through deliberate efforts. Living with this intention transforms mundane activities into opportunities for spiritual growth and influence. It's a commitment to continually refine our character, seeking to mirror Christ in all we do, no matter how routine the task may seem. Realizing this empowers us to embrace each day with purpose and passion.

Moreover, the concept of identity is foundational to kingdom living. (Living the Abundant Life Jesus Promised, n.d.). Our true identity is rooted in who God says we are, rather than external influences or personal insecurities. Embracing this new, divine identity shifts how we perceive challenges and opportunities. We grow bolder in our pursuits, knowing we act not out of fear but from a place of security and assurance in God's promises.

Legacy, in the context of kingdom living, extends beyond familial inheritance; it encompasses the spiritual and moral legacy we leave behind. It challenges us to evaluate the impact of our actions and how outsiders might perceive our faith through them. Ultimately, our goal is to pass on a legacy that embodies love, faith, and integrity— qualities that withstand time and trials.

To encourage readers, consider this: integrating these principles might initially feel like an uphill battle, but the resulting peace and fulfillment make the effort worthwhile. Striving for an abundant life defined by kingdom values not only enriches our lives but also profoundly influences others. Encouraging a broad adoption of such values invites a cultural shift toward endemic harmony and spiritual growth.

Ultimately, by striving to align every aspect of our lives with these biblical values, we reflect the Kingdom of God on Earth. It's a journey worth undertaking—a task that, although filled with hurdles, brings us closer to living out the fullness and richness that God intended for us. Our daily decision to live in accordance with God's

NEW LIFE   In 3 Priorities of TRIUMPH

principles not only builds our character but impacts the world around us, affirming that a life devoted to kingdom values is a life well-lived.

José E. Espinoza

Summary and Reflections

Now that we have explored the depths of understanding God's will, experiencing divine love, and recognizing His justice through the scriptures, it's clear that these principles are not just concepts but essential elements to embody in our daily lives. By developing habits of regular Bible study and prayer, we open ourselves to God's guidance and wisdom, allowing His voice to shape our decisions and actions. In doing so, we align our intentions with His purposes, experiencing a life transformed by His love and justice. Embracing these biblical teachings provides a roadmap for living a faith-centered life, where every choice reflects the values of the Kingdom of Heaven on Earth. As we move forward, let us commit to practicing these principles, fostering spiritual growth, and becoming vessels of God's love and justice in our communities. By doing so, we not only deepen our relationship with God but also inspire those around us, collectively building a world that reflects His divine kingdom.

NEW LIFE   In 3 Priorities of TRIUMPH

Reference List

Crowther, W. (2024, February 27). *Christianity's Perspective on Justice: Beliefs and Teachings*. Abundant Life Church | Coffs Harbour Church. https://alc.net.au/christianitys-perspective-on-justice-beliefs-and-teachings/

Charles, A. (2021, August 2). *Practical Prayers for Purpose and Direction in Your Life*. Live Inspired by Purpose. https://liveinspiredbypurpose.com/practical-prayers-for-purpose-and-direction-in-your-life/

Institute, C. S. L. (2018, December 8). *Discovering God's Purpose for Your Life*. C.S. Lewis Institute. https://www.cslewisinstitute.org/resources/discovering-gods-purpose-for-your-life/

Living the Abundant Life Jesus Promised. (n.d.). Matt Tommey Mentoring. https://www.matttommeymentoring.com/life_abundant.html

Mast, B., & Mast, B. (2019, December 20). *Building a Legacy - Be in Health*. Be in Health -. https://www.beinhealth.com/building-a-legacy/

José E. Espinoza

Part 3:

CONNECTED with The HOLY SPIRIT

José E. Espinoza

Chapter 7:

Accepting The Guidance of the Holy Spirit

Have you ever felt a longing for something more in your spiritual life, a thirst for a deeper connection with the divine that everyday routines fail to satisfy? Perhaps you've wondered why some believers experience an unshakeable peace and clarity, even amidst life's chaos, while others feel adrift in uncertainty. Is there a secret to unlocking this profound spiritual depth, or are such experiences reserved for only a select few? As you navigate your own faith journey, these questions might weigh heavily on your heart.

This chapter delves into the keys to embracing the guidance of the Holy Spirit, a vital step towards transforming your spiritual life. We will explore how baptism serves as a doorway to a Spirit-led existence and how it empowers believers to align more closely with God's will. By understanding the richness of living through the Holy Spirit, you'll uncover insights into how this divine presence can shape your daily decisions and fortify your faith, making you a true witness of God's love and purpose in your life.

Baptism and Divine Connection for Strength

Experiencing the fullness of the Holy Spirit through water baptism and the Holy Spirit baptism, begins the transformative journey into a Spirit-led life. For believers, baptism isn't just a solemn ritual; it serves as the entry point into a new spiritual pathway marked by guidance and illumination from the Holy Spirit. This act of faith represents both a commitment to following the teachings of Christ and a tangible expression of one's inner belief in the power of redemption and spiritual renewal. (Nyarko, 2024).

Baptism, especially the type carried out in Jesus' name, plays a critical role in reshaping one's spiritual identity. It symbolizes spiritual rebirth, purification, and the official transition into a community of faith. By submerging in water, a believer leaves behind the weight of past sins and emerges into a world filled with hope and divine purpose. (Gissel, 2023). This immersion represents the washing away of former transgressions, allowing the slate to be wiped clean as a precursor to receiving divine guidance. Fundamentally, baptism signals a readiness to accept the Spirit's calling and wisdom, aligning oneself more closely with God's will.

As a powerful initiation rite, baptism serves more than the function of cleansing. It is the foundational ritual that marks a believer's readiness to adopt a Spirit-led life, thereby shifting one's perceptions and values. The act itself channels the grace of the Holy Spirit into the individual's life, furnishing believers with newfound discernment and spiritual insights. These insights are crucial for living a life anchored in divine principles and for navigating the complexities of modern existence. By conferring the Holy Spirit's plenitude upon baptismal participants, this transformative act equips them to distinguish between worldly distractions and the essential truths of their faith.

Scriptural accounts underscore the profound impact of baptism in both symbolic and practical terms. For example, in the New Testament, Jesus' own baptism by John in the Jordan River serves as a pivotal moment in Christian narrative history. It was not merely a rite of passage but also a turning point that affirmed His divine mission and foreshadowed His sacrificial journey. (Nyarko, 2024). As the Holy Spirit descended upon Him, this moment embodied the transition from the old covenant to a new dispensation of spiritual grace, available to everyone willing to accept this divine gift. Similarly, Christians today see their own baptisms as recreating this transformative narrative, initiating them into a deeper relationship with Christ and His community.

The Holy Spirit's abundance in a believer's life, initiated through baptism, cannot be overstated. This divine presence is essential for the individual's spiritual evolution and growth, endowing them with spiritual gifts and fortitude. Post-baptismal life often leads to increased spiritual awareness and an ability to meet life's challenges with renewed strength. The role of the Holy Spirit in this context is akin to an ongoing conversation between the divine and the individual, offering guidance, wisdom, and a framework for understanding God's will in everyday life. (Gissel, 2023).

Baptism serves a dual purpose. While it is a personal expression of faith, it also brings individuals into a community bound by shared beliefs and commitment to living out God's teachings. This community aspect cannot be overlooked, for it is within these circles of faith that individuals find mutual support, spiritual nourishment, and collective witness to the power of the Holy Spirit in their lives. By participating in shared experiences and testimonies, believers reinforce their dedication to God's standards and become emboldened witnesses of their faith journeys.

Through baptism, believers step into a more profound and fulfilling existence that aligns with divine teachings and intentions. It readies them for the subsequent interaction with the Holy Spirit, an essential component for further spiritual empowerment and growth. The infusion of the Holy Spirit in their lives encourages a lifestyle shift that manifests in various ways, from ethical choices to compassionate behaviors and transformative community involvement.

NEW LIFE In 3 Priorities of TRIUMPH

The next step in this spiritual journey emphasizes the concept of the Holy Spirit's plenitude. Or what many Pentecostal Christians call; **'The Baptism of/in The Holy Spirit'.** This forthcoming exploration focuses on how the fullness of the Holy Spirit fosters deeper personal and spiritual transformations, resulting in a richer understanding of God's will. The abundance of the Holy Spirit acts as a catalyst for change and development, urging believers toward a continuous journey of faith and an ever-expanding grasp of divine purpose. It's a commitment to ongoing spiritual evolution and the realization that, through the Holy Spirit's presence, one can achieve greater enlightenment and comprehension of their ordained path in life. This seamless transition into exploring the plentitude of the Holy Spirit paves the way for a comprehensive embrace of spiritual ideals and further cements the foundational role of baptism in the overarching narrative of Christian faith.

José E. Espinoza

Baptism (Fullness) of The Holy Spirit for Everyday Discernment and Ministry, and triumph

Baptism of the Holy Spirit in each of us, marks the beginning of a Spirit-led life, opening up a transformative journey through the guidance of the Holy Spirit. It paves the way for spiritual empowerment, illuminating one's divine purpose. This initiation creates a foundation where believers are invited to experience the Holy Spirit's fullness, which brings profound change in both personal and spiritual dimensions, shaping their lives to reflect God's will more deeply.

Understanding the concept of the Holy Spirit's plentitude, starts with recognizing the empowerment it provides. The Holy Spirit serves not only as a source of spiritual vitality but also as a dynamic force that catalyzes personal growth and transformation. According to the teachings of John, the **Spirit leads believers into a deeper relationship with Christ and His teachings**, offering a life that overflows with purpose and peace, producing the fruit of the Spirit like love, joy, peace, patience, kindness, goodness, faithfulness, gentleness, and self-control.

140

NEW LIFE   In 3 Priorities of TRIUMPH

(**Galatians 5:22-23**). (Have You Made the Wonderful Discovery of the Spirit-Filled Life? | Cru, 2025). Such attributes emerge naturally when one is filled with and directed by the Holy Spirit, further enhancing the believer's ability to discern God's will and live accordingly.

Moreover, the Holy Spirit empowers believers to serve others more effectively, fostering a greater sense of connection with and responsibility towards their community. With the Spirit's guidance, believers can discern the needs around them with clarity and respond with sincerity and compassion. For instance, believers may find themselves more attuned to the struggles and pain of others, inspiring them to engage in acts of service that address these needs. Whether it be organizing community outreach programs, volunteering at local shelters, or simply extending a hand of friendship to someone in need, the Spirit inspires such actions that reflect Christ's love and mercy.

The effectiveness of this service is rooted in the Spirit's ability to foster genuine care and a proactive approach to addressing the needs of those around us. Consider a believer who, inspired by the Holy Spirit, initiates a grassroots movement to support families dealing with food insecurity. This compassion-driven action not only provides tangible assistance to those in need but also serves as a testament to the power of the Holy Spirit working through the believer's life, reflecting God's love in action.

The fullness of the Holy Spirit also enhances spiritual awareness, allowing believers to perceive God's work in everyday life more acutely. This heightened awareness transforms ordinary events into components of a divine narrative, helping believers recognize everyday miracles occurring through simple acts of kindness or unexpected moments of connection. For example, a chance encounter with a stranger could lead to a profound conversation that uplifts both individuals, reminding them of God's presence in their lives. Such instances reinforce faith and foster gratitude, emphasizing the continuous blessings God bestows upon His people.

This recognition of divine intervention in daily life strengthens one's faith. It adds depth to the believer's spiritual journey, making each day an opportunity to witness God's hand at work and respond with praise and thanksgiving. It's a cycle of receiving and giving that enriches both the personal and community aspects of a believer's life.

As believers continue to grow in their understanding of the Spirit's role, they become increasingly aware of the importance of sharing personal testimonies of God's love. These testimonies serve as powerful evangelistic tools, showcasing real-life applications of faith and how it becomes a transformative force. For instance, sharing stories of how one's life has been touched by God's grace or how prayer provided guidance can resonate deeply with others, fostering genuine connections that can lead others to explore their spiritual journeys.

Offering these personal stories is crucial for spreading the Gospel, as it allows others to see the tangible effects of faith in action. Similar to how the apostles were moved by the Spirit to spread the message of Christ through their firsthand experiences, today's believers can do the same by sharing their narratives. Such personal accounts can bridge cultural and generational divides, demonstrating the universality of God's love and the relatable, human aspects of spiritual growth.

This exploration transitions smoothly into discussing the broader relevance of these stories, not just for personal edification but as a tool for broader evangelistic efforts in sharing the Gospel's light. Next, we will delve deeper into how these testimonies inspire others, creating a ripple effect of faith that extends beyond individual experiences. By sharing these personal experiences, believers not only strengthen their own faith but also contribute to the spiritual growth of others, fulfilling Christ's command to be witnesses of His love and truth.

Throughout this section, the emphasis has been on illuminating how the Holy Spirit's empowerment enriches the believer's life in various forms—from personal transformation to community engagement, heightened spiritual awareness, and effective evangelization through personal testimonies. (The Holy Spirit, 2025). Experiencing the fullness of the Holy Spirit not only brings an individual closer to God but empowers them to manifest His love and purpose in the world actively. As this understanding becomes clearer, believers can better appreciate their role in God's grand narrative, supporting one another in faith and action.

NEW LIFE In 3 Priorities of TRIUMPH

Testifying God's Love with Spiritual Awareness

Connecting the experiences of spiritual empowerment with personal testimonies may seem abstract at first. The previous section explored the idea of living fully through the Holy Spirit, harnessing this divine empowerment for daily life. Now, it's about stepping further, moving beyond the personal transformation fueled by the Holy Spirit, and sharing these transformative experiences as forms of evangelization. It's not merely recounting a personal change; it's about witnessing God's enduring love and inviting others to recognize the presence of the divine in their own lives.

Just as the Holy Spirit enriches individual faith, awakening a deeper awareness of God's daily work, so does it inspire believers to articulate these experiences. Testimonies become a bridge to communicate God's love tangibly. Laurie. (2024) illuminates this connection when he emphasizes your story as a strategic tool—an entry point into broader conversations about faith. This aspect of storytelling aligns deeply with our desire to proclaim God's deeds, which becomes more than witnessing; it's about being a beacon of hope to those searching for meaning and guidance.

Personal testimonies stand as vivid illustrations that help others connect with spiritual truths. Abstract theology and doctrines can often alienate, yet a firsthand account brimming with emotion and personal insight can cut through uncertainty and skepticism. It's the authenticity in these stories, as supported by James (2024), which can encourage faith and spark dialogue. The practice of sharing personal stories offers a chance to demonstrate how God's love and power manifest in everyday situations.

Consider how testimonies serve as catalysts for spiritual awakening. A believer recounting their journey might share how the Holy Spirit provided clarity during a life-changing decision or strength during a moment of weakness. These stories resonate because they are real, relatable demonstrations of God's intervention. James (2024) asserts that such narratives are not self-centered; instead, they glorify God and serve as compelling invitations for others to explore their spiritual potential.

Referencing the Gospels, one finds ample examples of testimonies where Jesus' life and mission transform lives. These narratives, steeped in divine acts and teachings, offer parallel insights into individual experiences of faith today. The Gospels themselves, as testimonies, affirm the power in sharing one's personal encounters with God. This act of sharing—whether through recounting a miraculous healing or a moment of revelation—bridges ancient wisdom with contemporary experiences, emphasizing the timelessness of God's love (James, 2024).

Personal stories also foster community among believers, helping to build bonds through collective celebration and reflection on God's work. As people share their stories, they encourage and strengthen one another's faith. This communal aspect of testimony sharing showcases a powerful ripple effect whereby one story can catalyze multiple awakenings and conversions, mirroring the transformative power of the Holy Spirit discussed in the previous section.

Moreover, these stories challenge doubts and build faith not through forceful argumentation but by modeling authentic, lived experiences of faith. Laurie (2024) highlights how personal testimonies encourage a shift from darkness to light, motivating others to explore God's promise of hope and redemption. The power of these stories lies in their ability to make faith accessible and desirable.

Scripture offers numerous examples of these transitions. From Paul's radical transformation after his Damascus encounter to King David's songs of deliverance, biblical testimonies speak to individual change that ripples outward, impacting others (James, 2024). These stories become a testament to God's enduring faithfulness, inviting believers today to become living testimonies of divine love and action.

Encouraging believers to share their testimonies demands clarity and purpose, ensuring each narrative centers not just on personal victory but ultimately on God's redemptive power. Outlining how personal testimonies tie into the mission of the church offers a comprehensive view. They're not just heartwarming stories; they are divinely inspired accounts of God's active presence in our lives. This powerful tool for evangelization speaks directly to the heart, invoking joy, gratitude, and a call to embrace faith anew.

While these narratives may vary in detail and drama, their intrinsic value lies in their authenticity and their ability to unify believers in the shared experience of God's love. Personal testimonies reaffirm identity in Christ, reflecting the transformation from old to new, and offering fresh perspectives on God's unfolding narrative in the world (James, 2024).

In embracing this practice, believers not only affirm their faith but inspire others towards spiritual reflection and potential conversion. This aspect of personal sharing, when coupled with a focus on glorifying God, offers a holistic approach to living out the great commission—touched upon in the previous teaching on spiritual empowerment (Laurie, 2024).

In conclusion, personal testimonies intertwine individual transformation with the broader mission of the faith community. They provide evidence of God's ongoing work, offering hope and reassurance through their engaging narratives. Therefore, embracing the power of personal testimony is not merely an act of faith—it is a fundamental aspect of our divine calling, bridging personal transformation with the mission of evangelization, rooted **in the wisdom and empowerment of the Holy Spirit.**

José E. Espinoza

Summary and Reflections

This chapter highlights the pivotal role of baptism as a gateway to a Spirit-led life, igniting a transformative journey empowered by the Holy Spirit. Through this profound act of faith, believers embark on a path that reshapes their spiritual identity, aligning them with God's will and purpose. Baptism symbolizes rebirth and purification, serving as a foundation for deepening one's relationship with Christ. As we recognize the Holy Spirit's presence, we gain wisdom and discernment crucial for navigating life's challenges with divine guidance. Sharing personal testimonies becomes an essential witness to God's love, inviting others to explore their spiritual journeys. Now, with a deeper understanding of baptism and the Holy Spirit's empowerment, we can embrace our calling to live authentically and share our stories, inspiring others to experience the fullness of God's grace and community. This awareness not only enriches our spiritual journey but also strengthens our ability to be effective witnesses of faith, fostering a ripple effect that extends God's love beyond individual experiences and into the world.

*Conviction of being Saved:

With **The *Holy Spirit** *<u>Connected</u> in The Kingdom of God

-       <u>John 14:</u> 12-14. ~ 16-18. ~ 22-23. ~ 26-27.

José E. Espinoza

Reference List

Gissel, J. (2023, October 16). *The Apostolic Blueprint for Salvation: Repentance, Holy Spirit, Baptism, Faith and Works Explored - Pentecostal Publishing House Blog.* Pentecostal Publishing House Blog. https://blog.pentecostalpublishing.com/2023/10/16/the-apostolic-blueprint-for-salvation-repentance-holy-spirit-baptism-faith-and-works-explored/

Have You Made the Wonderful Discovery of the Spirit-Filled Life? | Cru. (2025). Cru.org. https://www.cru.org/us/en/train-and-grow/spiritual-growth/the-spirit-filled-life.html

James, J. (2024, December 7). *The Importance of Our Testimony - Shammah Outreach Movement.* Shammah Outreach Movement. https://shammahoutreachmovement.com/the-importance-of-our-testimony/

Laurie, G. (2024, October 8). *Evangelism and Your Personal Story.* Outreachmagazine.com. https://outreachmagazine.com/features/evangelism/57689-evangelism-and-your-personal-story.html

Nyarko, E. (2024, July 6). *Understanding the Christian Sacrament of Baptism: Perspectives of Some New Testament Personalities.* European Journal of Theology and Philosophy. https://doi.org/10.24018/theology.2024.4.3.131

The Holy Spirit. (2025). Gracegems.org. https://gracegems.org/Pink/holy_spirit.htm

Chapter 8:

Baptized & Filled with The Holy Spirit for Discipleship & Spiritual Growth

Have you ever wondered what it truly means to be **baptized in the Holy Spirit**? For many, this experience is shrouded in mystery and profound awe. It marks a turning point, often described as a powerful entry into a deeper, **more intimate walk with Christ**. Yet, questions linger. How does this baptism impact our journey as disciples? What role does it play in our spiritual growth and our ability to fulfill our calling? For those who are newly committed to their faith or exploring Christianity, understanding the Holy Spirit's purpose can seem like navigating uncharted waters.

In this chapter, we delve into these questions, providing clarity and guidance for young believers seeking to deepen their relationship with the Holy Spirit. By examining the pathway of discipleship and spiritual growth through the lens of being baptized and filled by the Spirit, we aim to illuminate how this divine partnership empowers us to live out the teachings of Jesus, engage with Scripture, and boldly share the Gospel—all while nurturing personal and communal spiritual maturity.

Deepening the Discipleship Path in the Fulness of the Holy Spirit

Baptism in the Holy Spirit marks the beginning of an exhilarating and sometimes challenging journey. It's not just a single event, but a life-altering invitation to deepen one's faith. This transformation requires **active partnership with the Holy Spirit**. After baptism, many believers notice how their commitment grows as they engage deeper with the Holy Spirit. It's a transformative relationship, much like nurturing any important relationship in our lives, that requires attention and deliberate action. **Romans 12:2** says, *"Do not conform to the pattern of this* *world, but be <u>transformed by the renewing of your mind</u>. Then you will be able to test and approve what God's will is—his good, pleasing and perfect will."*

For many, spiritual growth post-baptism begins with a renewed commitment to Scripture. Continuing to learn through Scripture is a cornerstone of spiritual expansion. Setting aside regular times for Bible study infuses everyday life with spiritual insights and guidance, enhancing one's understanding of God's word. Attending Bible study groups weekly or even attending an online class or seminar can open up new perspectives and spark inspiration that furthers personal spiritual journeys. The engagement with Scripture doesn't just expand the mind; it invigorates the soul and grounds believers in divine truth. **Psalm 119:105** reminds us, *"Your word is a lamp for my feet, a light on my path."*

Central to this spiritual journey is the practice of prayer. Consistent prayer acts as a lifeline, strengthening the connection between the believer, God, and the Holy Spirit. Many find keeping a prayer journal beneficial, capturing thoughts, reflections, and the answers to prayers that emerge over time. Another practice is setting a prayer routine, such as starting and ending each day with prayer, which seamlessly integrates faith into daily rhythms. For some, it could involve meditative silence, allowing oneself to be still and open to the Spirit's gentle whisper. **Philippians 4:6** instructs, *"Do not be anxious about anything, but in everything by prayer and supplication with thanksgiving let your requests be made known to God."*

Belonging to a faith community enriches this journey further. Communities of other believers serve as crucial anchors, providing encouragement and accountability. Faith groups, church gatherings, or fellowship events offer spaces where believers can share their spiritual experiences and learn from one another. Community creates spaces where wounds can heal, joy multiplies, and doubts find resolution in shared faith and wisdom. An example might be a **small group gathering,** where intimate settings encourage open dialogue and personal growth. **Hebrews 10:24-25** states, *"And let us consider how we may spur one another on toward love and good deeds, not giving up meeting together, as some are in the habit of doing, but encouraging* *one another—and all the more as you see the Day approaching."*

Within a community, discipleship emerges as an ongoing path marked by the Holy Spirit's guidance. Unlike a static state, it is dynamic and evolving, where each step brings new insights and deeper understanding. It's about seeing discipleship not as an arrival at a destination but as a part of a lifelong adventure full of learning, acquiring wisdom, and responding to the Spirit's leading. Participating in discipleship programs or mentorships helps individuals realize their potential in fulfilling the Great Commission, preparing them to inspire others with their faith journey. **Matthew 28:19-20** urges, *"Therefore go and make disciples of all nations, baptizing them in the name of the Father and of the Son and of the Holy Spirit, and teaching them to obey everything I have commanded you. And surely I am with you always, to the very end of the age."*

José E. Espinoza

Living out Jesus' Teachings

Following Jesus means living out His teachings in everyday actions. Studying Jesus' life in the Gospel reveals not just who Jesus was, but how we, too, might live today. Jesus taught the power of love, compassion, and humility, drawing examples from healing the sick to comforting the marginalized. His actions reminded us to see and serve the world through a lens of boundless compassion and empathy. Incorporating these lessons means acting with love, showing kindness even when it isn't easy, and choosing forgiveness over resentment. **John 13:34-35** says, *"A new command I give you: Love one another. As I have loved you, so you must love one another. By this everyone will know that you are my disciples, if you love one another."*

Practical steps to embody Jesus' teachings might include volunteering in community service, reaching out to someone in need, or simply taking the time to listen deeply to others. Jesus' life also emphasized the significance of prayer and seeking God's will, reflecting a life led by divine guidance and purposeful intention. By understanding that each day offers a new canvas to paint with deeds of kindness and love, believers can truly live out their faith. **Matthew 5:14-16**tells us, *"You are the light of the world. A town built on a hill cannot be hidden. Neither do people light a lamp and put it under a bowl. Instead they put it on its stand, and it gives light to everyone in the house. In the same way, let your light shine before others, that they may see your good deeds and glorify your Father in heaven."*

Support Systems and Expanding the Kingdom Through Service

Building on the foundation of continual spiritual growth and commitment to Christ's teachings, we step into the role of discipleship as a living, breathing journey. This journey is about more than personal edification; it's the very heartbeat of a life transformed by the Holy Spirit. When young adults and new believers embrace this dynamic, they set the stage to partake in God's mission— expanding His Kingdom through service and community engagement. **Romans 12:11-13**advises, *"Never be lacking in zeal, but keep your spiritual fervor, serving the Lord. Be joyful in hope, patient in affliction, faithful in prayer.*

José E. Espinoza

Share with the Lord's people who are in need. Practice hospitality."

A Spirit-filled life doesn't just remain within; it propels believers outward to extend love. Transformative power resides in acts of service. Whether locally or globally, these endeavors show faith in action. In many form possible. Sharing the love and message of Christ—this is ministry lived out. Such projects are not just about physical transformation but are platforms for dialogue, venues where the faith story gets told naturally and compellingly. **1 Peter 4:10** states, *"Each of you should use whatever gift you have received to serve others, as faithful stewards of God's grace in its various forms."*

A vibrant example can be seen in local food drives. Imagine a church congregation partnering with community organizations to address hunger. As boxes of canned goods and fresh produce get distributed to families in need, relationships form. Volunteers share conversations that move past surface-level exchanges, entering meaningful dialogues about hope, providence, and the Wholeness found in Christ. Such encounters multiply as they're repeated, each act of service another thread woven into the fabric of God's outreach. **Proverbs 19:17** tells us, *"Whoever is kind to the poor lends to the Lord, and he will reward them for what they have done."*

Ministry thrives on collaboration. When individuals join forces under the Holy Spirit's guidance, they extend their reach and impact. Consider an urban area where multiple churches band together to tackle homelessness. They pool resources to offer shelter, meals, and job preparation programs. These cooperative efforts, filled with guidance from the Holy Spirit, equip them to do more together than they could alone. These partnerships become tangible expressions of Christ's teachings on community and service. **Ecclesiastes 4:9** says, *"Two are better than one, because they have a good return for their labor."*

Furthermore, service initiatives offer practical ways to live out discipleship. Take mission trips, for example. Believers travel to different parts of the world, sometimes in difficult and demanding conditions, equipped only with a servant's heart. They engage in building schools, teaching classes, or providing medical care. Here, faith is made visible, and service intersects with storytelling, naturally showcasing the love of Christ. The mission trips often lead to reciprocal blessings, as those serving learn from the communities they aim to help. **Acts 1:8** tells us, *"But you will receive power when the Holy Spirit comes on you; and you will be my witnesses in Jerusalem, and in all Judea and Samaria, and to the ends of the earth."*

Church initiatives, too, play a significant role. Community-focused events, like back-to-school drives or neighborhood fairs, become more than social gatherings. They are opportunities to establish trust, foster relationships, and make the presence of God's Kingdom tangible to outsiders. In showing up consistently for their community, believers earn the credibility necessary for their message to resonate. **Galatians 6:9-10** encourages, *"Let us not become weary in doing good, for at the proper time we will reap a harvest if we do not give up. Therefore, as we have opportunity, let us do good to all people, especially to those who belong to the family of believers."*

Another key aspect is the role of personal witness in these efforts. When believers share their testimonies through acts of service, they offer a unique and personal perspective on what it means to live a Spirit-filled life. Picture an individual who, after a significant conversion experience, channels their new-found energy into setting up a mentorship program for at-risk youth. This initiative doesn't just address immediate needs— it tells a story of transformation and conveys the ongoing journey of discipleship. **1 Timothy 4:12 Galatians 5:22-23** reminds us, *"But the fruit of the Spirit is love, joy, peace, forbearance, kindness, goodness, faithfulness, gentleness and self-control. Against such things there is no law."*

To maximize the impact of these efforts, clear and specific examples serve as poignant illustrations. When one sees the tangible impact of service— such as a local family experiencing relief from chronic food insecurity due to a church's consistent outreach—there's a clarion call to continue these efforts. Avoiding repetitiveness in these examples helps maintain the freshness and clarity of the narrative, underscoring each story's unique contribution to the larger picture. **James 2:17** says, *"In the same way, faith by itself, if it is not accompanied by action, is dead."*

The path of **discipleship**, framed **by the Holy Spirit's guidance**, <u>leads believers to find meaning and purpose in service</u>. **It's an ongoing growth**

process that molds and shapes one's spiritual journey. Far more than individual acts, service becomes a communal expression of faith, fostering unity and understanding among diverse groups. Each collaborative effort and ministry partnership extends an invitation to partake in God's ever-expanding Kingdom. **1 Corinthians 12:27** tells us, *"Now you are the body of Christ, and each one of you is a part of it."*

Believers, emboldened by the Holy Spirit, step out into the world, carrying God's message. Service reflects not just the teachings of Christ but His very essence. It's a call to action, a fulfillment of the mission to share His love. By showing up in these spaces, believers make the abstract tangible, the spiritual visible. They contribute to a larger legacy, as every good deed and every shared story magnifies God's presence in our world. **Matthew 5:16** reminds us, *"In the same way, let your light shine before others, that they may see your good deeds and glorify your Father in heaven."*

NEW LIFE   In 3 Priorities of TRIUMPH

Summary & Reflections (of the 1st Part of Chapter 8)

In understanding the profound significance of being baptized in the Holy Spirit, we embrace a holy purpose that reshapes every aspect of our spiritual journey. It's a call to deepen our faith in Jesus and fulfill the Great Commission as a personal invitation to boldly share the Gospel and serve fearlessly in expanding God's Kingdom. By integrating practices such as prayer, scripture study, and active participation in faith communities, we lay the groundwork for ongoing discipleship, allowing the Holy Spirit to guide us every step of the way. This transformative path equips us to embody Jesus' teachings through daily actions, fostering love, compassion, and humility. As we navigate this vibrant journey, we are empowered to influence others, enriching not only our own lives but also the broader community. The next steps involve engaging with church initiatives and service projects, which will reinforce our commitment to live out our faith practically and propagate God's love beyond the confines of the church. Together, let us embark on this dynamic adventure, where our growing relationship with the Holy Spirit serves as both a beacon of hope and a catalyst for change, ensuring that our spiritual life reflects the vitality and purpose found within God's eternal mission. **John 15:5** reminds us, *"I am the vine; you are the branches. <u>If you remain in me and I in you, you will bear much fruit;</u> apart from me you can do nothing."*

NEW LIFE   In 3 Priorities of TRIUMPH

Reinforcement (Biblically) as a 2nd Part of this chapter:

Baptized and Filled with the Holy Spirit for Discipleship and Spiritual Growth

Chapter Summary

In this chapter, we had already explored the holy purpose of being baptized in the Holy Spirit, the journey of deepening one's faith in Jesus, and the personal calling every believer has to fulfill in the Great Commission. Emphasizing the importance of boldly sharing the Gospel and serving others as a means to expand The Kingdom of God in our present environment.

Now, let's do it reinforcing each topic with Biblical Scripture 'citations' for doctrinal instruction, 'truth, and veracity'.

José E. Espinoza

Deepening the Discipleship Path in the Fulness of the Holy Spirit

Commitment to Growth

Connected with the Holy Spirit and post-baptismal commitment to deepening faith and following Jesus, our spiritual journey is guided by continual learning through Scripture, regular prayer, and engagement with a faith community.

Scripture Reference:

· 2 Timothy 3:16-17: **"All Scripture (Bible) is God**-breathed **(by The Holy Spirit)** and is useful for teaching, rebuking, correcting and training in righteousness, so that the servant of God may be thoroughly equipped for every good work."

· 1 Thessalonians 5:17: **"Pray without ceasing."**

· Hebrews 10:24-25: "And let us consider how we may spur one another on toward love and good deeds, not giving up meeting together, as some are in the habit of doing, but **encouraging one another**—and all the more as **you see the Day approaching."**

NEW LIFE   In 3 Priorities of   TRIUMPH

Through continuous learning and engagement, believers grow spiritually, strengthening their personal relationship with God.

Long-term Vision

Understanding discipleship as a lifelong journey guided by the Holy Spirit involves recognizing that spiritual growth is an ongoing process. Believers must be open to the Holy Spirit's guidance in different life seasons and set long-term goals to maintain focus on their faith development.

Scripture Reference:

· Philippians 1:6: "Being confident of this, that he who began a good work in you will carry it on to completion until the day of Christ Jesus."

· Romans 8:14: "For those who are led by the Spirit of God are the children of God."

Following Jesus

Discipleship involves emulating the life and teachings of Christ. Studying Jesus' actions provides a model for daily living, practicing love and compassion reflects Christ's character, and committing to ethical principles derived from His teachings shapes behavior.

Scripture Reference:

· John 13:15: "I have set you an example that you should do as I have done for you."

· Ephesians 5:1-2: "Follow God's example, therefore, as dearly loved children and walk in the way of love, just as Christ loved us and gave himself up for us as a fragrant offering and sacrifice to God."

Support Systems

The Church provides community and support for spiritual growth. Small groups offer a platform for sharing experiences and insights, access to **mentorship** fosters personal and spiritual development, and church initiatives create opportunities for communal worship and service.

Scripture Reference:

· Galatians 6:2: "Carry each other's burdens, and in this way you will fulfill the law of Christ."

NEW LIFE   In 3 Priorities of TRIUMPH

· 1 Corinthians 12:27: "Now you are the body of Christ, and each one of you is a part of it."

The Great Commission as Personal Vocation; Jesus' Directive & Command

Emphasizes the importance of Jesus' command to spread the Gospel, understanding this command shapes the believer's purpose, highlights the collective responsibility of all Christians, and reflecting on the urgency of the directive inspires proactive engagement.

Scripture Reference:

· Matthew 28:19-20: "Therefore go and make disciples of all nations, baptizing them in the name of the **Father** and of the **Son** and of the **Holy Spirit**, and teaching them to obey everything I have commanded you. And surely I am with you always, to the very end of the age."

Purpose and Identity

Fulfilling this call becomes a defining aspect of Christian identity, embracing this commission as

José E. Espinoza

integral to one's faith journey, recognizing the transformative impact on personal and communal identity, and fostering a sense of belonging within the wider body of Christ.

Scripture Reference:

· 1 Peter 2:9: "But you are a chosen people, a royal priesthood, a holy nation, God's special possession, that you may declare the praises of him who called you out of darkness into his wonderful light."

Empowerment by Holy Spirit

The Holy Spirit empowers believers to overcome challenges, providing wisdom and discernment in challenging situations, promoting courageous decision-making, and instilling confidence to share testimonies and experiences.

Scripture Reference:

· Acts 1:8: "But you will receive power when the Holy Spirit comes on you; and you will be my witnesses in Jerusalem, and in all Judea and Samaria, and to the ends of the earth."

NEW LIFE   In 3 Priorities of TRIUMPH

· 2 Timothy 1:7: "For the Spirit God gave us does not make us timid, but gives us power, love and self-discipline."

Global Reach

Personal calling also implies reaching beyond one's immediate community, cultivating a global perspective, understanding the importance of international missions, and supporting global initiatives as a commitment to the universal church.

Scripture Reference:

· Mark 16:15: "He said to them, 'Go into all the world and preach the gospel to all creation.'"

José E. Espinoza

Announcing the Good News with Boldness

Courage in Faith

The Spirit emboldens believers to share the Gospel without fear, developing boldness requires stepping outside comfort zones, testimonials of others can inspire confidence in one's outreach, and prayer increases reliance on the Spirit for strength and courage.

Scripture Reference:

· 1 Corinthians 16:13: "Be on your guard; stand firm in the faith; be courageous; be strong."

· Acts 4:31: "After they prayed, the place where they were meeting was shaken. And they were all filled with the Holy Spirit and spoke the word of God boldly."

Clarity of Message

Ensures believers communicate the message of salvation clearly, understanding core truths helps articulate beliefs effectively, avoiding jargon makes the message accessible to diverse audiences, and practicing methods for sharing the Gospel enhances communication skills.

Scripture Reference:

· Colossians 4:6: "Let your conversation be always full of grace, seasoned with salt, so that you may know how to answer everyone."

· 1 Peter 3:15: "But in your hearts revere Christ as Lord. Always be prepared to give an answer to everyone who asks you to give the reason for the hope that you have. But do this with gentleness and respect."

Ambassadorship

Christians act as **ambassadors** of Christ's message around the world, representing Christ serves as a powerful testimony to non-believers, taking part in outreach programs showcases commitment to evangelism, and living authentically in faith reinforces the validity of the message shared.

Scripture Reference:

· 2 Corinthians 5:20: "We are therefore Christ's ambassadors, as though God were making his appeal through us. We implore you on Christ's behalf: Be reconciled to God."

Scriptural Guidance

Biblical passages underpin the bold announcement of the Gospel, familiarity with Scripture reinforces confidence in sharing, using Scriptural examples cultivates deeper conversations, and memorizing key verses equips believers for spontaneous sharing moments.

Scripture Reference:

· Romans 10:17: "Consequently, faith comes from hearing the message, and the message is heard through the word about Christ."

· Psalm 119:105: "Your word is a lamp for my feet, a light on my path."

NEW LIFE   In 3 Priorities of TRIUMPH

Expanding the Kingdom in the Spirit Through Service

Community Engagement

Service in local church and global communities as a Gospel tool, volunteering in our church demonstrates tangible expressions of faith, collaborative projects unite believers for a common cause, and engaging with the community fosters relationships and builds trust.

Scripture Reference:

· James 2:14-17: "What good is it, my brothers and sisters, if someone claims to have faith but has no deeds? Can such faith save them? Suppose a brother or a sister is without clothes and daily food. If one of you says to them, 'Go in peace; keep warm and well fed,' but does nothing about their physical needs, what good is it? In the same way, faith by itself, if it is not accompanied by action, is dead."

· Galatians 5:13: "You, my brothers and sisters, were called to be free. But do not use your freedom to indulge the flesh; rather, serve one another humbly in love."

Manifesting Christ's Love

Through acts of service, believers demonstrate God's love. Each act of kindness serves as a reflection of Christ's love, genuine love captures the attention of those who may be skeptical, and service opens pathways to meaningful conversations about faith.

Scripture Reference:

· 1 John 3:18: "Dear children, let us not love with words or speech but with actions and in truth."

· Matthew 5:16: "In the same way, let your light shine before others, that they may see your good deeds and glorify your Father in heaven."

Collaborative Ministry

Partnering with others, led by the Holy Spirit, to amplify the impact of service for the Kingdom. Working alongside different organizations maximizes outreach potential, sharing resources enhances effectiveness and reach of ministry efforts, and collective prayer for initiatives strengthens unity and purpose.

Scripture Reference:

· Ecclesiastes 4:9-12: "Two are better than one, because they have a good return for their labor: If either of them falls down, one can help the other up. But pity anyone who falls and has no one to help them up. Also, if two lie down together, they will keep warm. But how can one keep warm alone? Though one may be overpowered, two can defend themselves. A cord of three strands is not quickly broken."

· 1 Corinthians 3:6-9: "I planted the seed, Apollos watered it, but God has been making it grow. So neither the one who plants nor the one who waters is anything, but only God, who makes things grow. The one who plants and the one who waters have one purpose, and they will each be rewarded according to their own labor. For we are co-workers in God's service; you are God's field, God's building."

José E. Espinoza

Summary and Reflections

The guidance of the Holy Spirit, the desire for discipleship, and the communion in the family of God, leads believers on a transformative journey of faith that expands the Kingdom of Heaven on earth. As we fulfill the Great Commission, share the Gospel boldly, and serve others; we glorify God's holy name, shining His light in a world clouded by darkness and in need of His love.

Scripture Reference:

· Matthew 5:14-16: **"You are the light of the world**. A town built on a hill cannot be hidden. Neither do people light a lamp and put it under a bowl. Instead they put it on its stand, and it gives light to everyone in the house. In the same way, let your light shine before others, that they may see your good deeds and glorify your Father in heaven."

Chapter 9:

Connected Family in The Spirit of God; to Fulfill Purpose in Unity

In today's world, where individualism often takes center stage, **finding one's place within a community can be a challenge**. A young adult person eager to deepen his or her faith, found himself or herself struggling with a sense of isolation upon **joining the local church**. Despite the warm smiles and cordial greetings, she or he may feel like an outsider, <u>with the uncertainty of how to connect with others on a deeper level</u>. Each Sunday, as members embraced during worship, she or he **yearned for that same sense of belonging**, but they might not be sure <u>how to bridge the gap between acquaintance and family in faith</u>.

José E. Espinoza

Hebrews 10:24-25 reminds us, *"And let us consider how we may spur one another on toward love and good deeds, not giving up meeting together, as some are in the habit of doing, but encouraging one another—and all the more as you see the Day approaching."*

For many new believers, this struggle highlights a pressing issue: how do we cultivate genuine unity and purpose within a spiritual community? Without strong bonds, even the most vibrant gatherings can feel empty and disconnected. In this chapter, we delve into these challenges, exploring the fundamental aspects of spiritual unity and collective purpose among believers. Through understanding the importance of community, collaboration, and a spirit-led lifestyle, we aim to uncover how believers can fulfill God's mission <u>as a unified royal family of the Kingdom of God.</u>

Bonding in God's Spiritual Family

In exploring the role of unity and fellowship among believers, it becomes evident that the Church stands as an extended family, bound together by shared faith and purpose. This family metaphor finds its depth in how believers, akin to family members, support one another through life's ebbs and flows. The Church, with its foundation rooted in love and acceptance, becomes a nurturing environment where spiritual growth and community relationships flourish. **Romans 12:5** states, *"so in Christ we, though many, form one body, and each member belongs to all the others."*

One of the most profound examples of this is celebrating baptisms. Baptisms are not merely personal milestones but communal experiences that undergird the unity and belonging within the Church family. As each believer emerges from the waters, they symbolically enter into this family, welcomed and affirmed by their spiritual community. Such ceremonies embody the essence of unity, as participants joyfully recognize the transformative power of faith and the commitment to support one another on the journey ahead. This shared joy and acknowledgment foster an enduring connection that far exceeds typical social bonds. **Galatians 3:27-28** tells us, *"for all of you who were baptized into Christ have clothed yourselves with Christ. There is neither Jew nor*

José E. Espinoza

Gentile, neither slave nor free, nor is there male and female, for you are all one in Christ Jesus. "

Shared testimonies play a significant role in this dynamic as well. By recounting personal faith experiences, believers not only testify to God's work in their lives but also strengthen communal bonds. Hearing each other's stories builds accountability and inspires others who may face similar challenges, promoting an atmosphere of trust and shared vulnerability. These narratives become threads that weave individuals into the collective tapestry of the Church, enhancing a sense of solidarity and empathy.

Witnessing the unfolding of each believer's journey further strengthens these bonds. During times of celebration and trials, the church family rallies together, providing emotional and spiritual support. This is often seen in accountability groups and prayer circles, where members commit to walk alongside one another, offering guidance and encouragement. These groups address the human need for connection and companionship, fostering personal growth and preventing the isolation that can occur in times of difficulty. **James 5:16** encourages, *"Therefore confess your sins to each other and pray for each other so that* *you may be healed. The prayer of a righteous person is powerful and effective. "*

These support systems also extend to practical aspects of life, addressing both spiritual and physical needs. Emotional support might manifest in visiting one another during illness, offering meals to families in crisis, or simply providing a listening ear and heartfelt prayer. Such actions are rooted in the biblical call to bear one another's burdens, creating an environment where each believer feels valued and understood. This tangible demonstration of care strengthens the unity of the Church, creating a real family experience characterized by sharing both joys and sorrows. **Galatians 6:2** reminds us, *"Carry each other's burdens, and in this way you will fulfill the law of Christ. "*

In this nurturing environment, individual testimonies, accountability, and acts of service coalesce to demonstrate the Church's role as God's extended family. The value of unity and fellowship is not in mere affiliation but in the authentic relationships that enrich the lives of its members. Through every challenge and milestone, the Church embodies a sanctuary of belonging, where differences become opportunities for deeper connection rather than sources of division.

The Church also models patience and grace, recognizing that unity does not necessitate uniformity. The early Christian community, as described in Scripture, was diverse in its makeup yet unified in purpose. This principle extends to contemporary believers, who, despite differing backgrounds and perspectives, are called to stand united in their mission. This diversity enriches the community, mirroring the multifaceted nature of the Body of Christ, where different members fulfill unique roles while serving a common goal. **Corinthians 12:12-13** states, *"Just as a body, though one, has many parts, but all its many parts form one body, so it is with Christ. For we were all baptized by one Spirit so as to form one body—whether Jews or Gentiles, slave or free— and we were all given the one Spirit to drink."*

The unity experienced within this spiritual family becomes foundational for collective mission endeavors. **Driven by the Holy Spirit,** the Church is equipped to extend its love and service beyond its walls, reaching out to the broader community with compassion and purpose. This external focus emphasizes that unity is not an end in itself but a precursor to fulfilling the Church's divine calling. The synergy of shared mission work exemplifies the power of collective participation, illustrating how working together can amplify impact far beyond individual efforts. **Acts 2:44-45** tells us, *"All the believers **were together and had everything in common**. They sold property and possessions to give to anyone who had need."*

As believers unite in service, they reflect Christ's love to those around them, effectively advancing God's kingdom and glorifying His name. This harmonious collaboration provides a powerful testimony to the world, demonstrating the transformative potential of faith when lived out in community. A family united not only edifies its own members but also inspires and draws others into its midst through its authenticity and love. **John 13:35** shares, ***"By this everyone will know that you are my disciples, if you love one another."***

By understanding and embracing this concept of familial unity, believers lay the groundwork for engaging in a spirit-led mission. As each member contributes their unique gifts and talents, the Church becomes an unstoppable force for good, navigating diverse challenges with resilience and grace. This unity, cultivated in love and sustained by purpose, holds the potential to reshape communities and lives, creating ripples of change that extend into eternity.

In this journey, the Church becomes a living testament to God's power and love, echoing the truth found in **Ecclesiastes—*"two are better than one because they stand stronger together"*.** (Edmonds, 2022). This strength in unity encourages believers to continue fostering environments that are welcoming and inclusive, where every person is valued as part of the family. As they do so, the Church not only fulfills its role internally but also becomes a beacon of hope and transformation in the world. Through unity and fellowship, the Church realizes its purpose, building God's kingdom with love, one relationship at a time.

Recognizing this deeper purpose, we pave the way to understand that unity among believers is just the beginning. In the coming sections, we will explore how these shared experiences and connections empower believers to engage in collaborative missions. These missions, inspired and guided by the Holy Spirit, underscore how unity is essential for advancing the Church's mission, demonstrating the exponential impact of working together to fulfill God's eternal purpose.

Collaborative Mission Guided by The Holy Spirit; for God's Glory

The discussion of unity and fellowship in the Church provides the groundwork for moving into a more dynamic phase: collaborative mission work. This transition is not merely theoretical but deeply practical, embodying the collective experience that comes with being part of a nurturing family. Just as families support one another, so too does the Church by encouraging believers as they engage in missions. This vision of the Church functions under the guidance of the Holy Spirit, empowering its members to work together in spreading the gospel and serving others.

When believers come together as a united body under the Spirit's direction, their collective mission becomes a more powerful force than isolated efforts. For instance, the early Church described in Acts demonstrates how shared outreach initiatives can exponentially increase their impact. As the Spirit filled the disciples gathered at Pentecost, they began to speak in tongues, reaching people from diverse backgrounds and cultures. (Saturation Church Planting, 2024). This moment marked the beginning of a widespread movement where the church's unity and the Spirit's guidance propelled their mission forward, setting a strong precedent for how collective action can result in significant transformations.

Such unity allows for diverse spiritual gifts to be harnessed effectively, creating a holistic mission approach. The realization that no one method or gift is sufficient on its own is essential. For example, the diverse methods of evangelism—ranging from personal interactions to audiovisual materials—reflect the manifold ways the Spirit uses believers to reach others. (EVANGELISM, 2023). Through individual and collective discernment, believers can identify and deploy their unique gifts in service to the mission, ensuring that efforts are not only complementary but also comprehensive. **1 Corinthians 12:4-6** mentions, *"There are different kinds of gifts, but the same Spirit distributes them. There are different kinds of service, but the same Lord. There are different kinds of working, but in all of* *them and in everyone it is the same God at work. "*

The Bible underscores the importance of these gifts, noting that each believer receives a manifestation of the Spirit for the common good. (**1 Corinthians 12:7**). This highlights the idea that each person, supported by the collective body, plays a crucial role in the Church's mission. By engaging in spiritual gift assessments and seeking affirmation from one another, believers can better understand their strengths and how to utilize them for God's kingdom. The process of identifying and implementing spiritual gifts emphasizes the need for believers to actively participate in ongoing spiritual development and community engagement.

The Antioch church, for instance, served as a model for how unified prayer and discernment led to the effective deployment of spiritual leaders. The church set apart Barnabas and Saul for mission work through the Holy Spirit's promptings, resulting in the spread of the gospel across various regions. (Saturation Church Planting, 2024). Such examples illustrate that prayer and planning play vital roles in unifying efforts and maximizing the impact of collective missions.

Collective prayer is an integral component that fosters unity within the Church, enhancing the collective mission's strength. By coming together in prayer, the Church invites the Spirit's transformative power, which aligns individual and communal efforts with divine will. This unity in purpose extends beyond immediate mission goals, instilling in believers a sense of shared destiny and responsibility to act as witnesses in all spheres of life. **Philippians 4:6-7** encourages, ***"Do not be anxious about anything, but in every situation, by prayer and petition, with thanksgiving, present your requests to God. And the peace of God, which transcends all understanding, will guard your hearts and your minds in Christ Jesus."***

Planning diverse methods of evangelism under the Spirit's guidance ensures that the Church remains adaptable and responsive to different contexts and cultures. Like a well-rehearsed symphony, each believer contributes their unique sound, creating a harmonious mission that speaks to the essence of the gospel. (EVANGELISM, 2023). By considering different approaches—such as community service, educational programs, and cultural exchanges—the Church can creatively and effectively share the message of Christ. Such diversity not only respects the uniqueness of each believer's gifts but also acknowledges the variety of needs within different communities. **1 Peter 4:10-11** states, *"Each of you should use whatever gift you have received to serve others, as faithful stewards of God's grace in its various forms. If anyone speaks, they should do so as one who speaks the very words of God. If anyone serves, they should do so with the strength God provides, so that in all things God may be praised through Jesus Christ. To him be the glory and the power for ever and ever. Amen."*

As we explore how a Spirit-led community collaborates in fulfilling divine purposes, it's important to recognize that this mission extends beyond church walls. It transforms how believers engage with their wider community, encouraging active participation in civic duties, social justice initiatives, and compassionate outreach. **Matthew 25:35-36** emphasizes, *"For I was hungry and you gave me something to eat, I was thirsty and you gave me something to drink, I was a stranger and you invited me in, I needed clothes and you* *clothed me, I was sick and you looked after me, I was in prison and you came to visit me."* This outward focus serves as a profound testament to the world of what it means to live a life reflective of Christ's love and mission.

Transitioning to the next section, "Leading a Spirit-Led Life," we can observe how personal and communal missions rooted in collective action significantly influence individual lives. Living within a community dedicated to fulfilling God's purpose encourages personal growth and aligns individual decisions with divine guidance. The Holy Spirit not only empowers collective efforts but also ignites a personal transformation that naturally extends to everyday choices and interactions.

In summary, the cooperative mission led by the Holy Spirit exemplifies how collective unity translates into a powerful force for fulfilling God's purposes. By actively engaging in the mission, believers not only contribute to the Church's growth but also experience personal enrichment and spiritual depth. This unified approach underscores the importance of each believer's role within the greater narrative, encouraging everyone to embrace their unique gifts and participate in the

NEW LIFE   In 3 Priorities of TRIUMPH

Church's mission with love, commitment, and creativity. As we delve into leading a Spirit-led life, we discover how these collective efforts bear fruit in individual lives, further entrenching the values of community and purpose in all aspects of our journey.

Living a Spirit-Led Life and Celebrating Growth

Living a Spirit-led life takes center stage when it comes to making impactful personal decisions and benefiting the community. This approach plays an essential role in the shared mission among believers by fostering a deep sense of spiritual unity and purpose. Within the family of faith, each individual's walk with the Holy Spirit is instrumental in enhancing the collective mission. This requires each person to align their life more closely with the Holy Spirit, ensuring that every action contributes to the greater good.

Understanding the influence of the Holy Spirit starts with knowing His role—as a **Helper, Comforter**, and source of wisdom for every believer, working tirelessly to guide individuals in navigating daily challenges and decisions. **John**

14:26 states, *"But the Advocate, <u>the Holy Spirit,</u> whom the Father will send in my name, <u>will teach you all things and will remind you</u> of everything I have said to you."* By embracing His presence through constant prayer and reverence, believers learn to trust and lean into His divine support. (How the Holy Spirit Can Ignite Your Ordinary Life, 2015). From mundane choices like interactions at work to more significant, life-altering decisions, the Spirit offers comfort and guidance, effectively ensuring that every step taken resonates with God's will.

Moreover, it provides a framework for positively altering the dynamics of communal living. When believers are united by the Holy Spirit, they build an environment that thrives on mutual support and care. In essence, as each person strengthens their personal relationship with God, they inadvertently enrich their connection with others. These dynamic forms a robust support network, promoting a collective mission for the glory of God. (Tarrants, 2016). Collaborative initiatives, rooted in the Spirit's guidance, often bear witness to the outpouring of divine love, thereby drawing others into the fold of faith. **Acts 4:32** shares, *"All the believers were one in heart and mind. No one* *claimed that any of their possessions was their own, but they shared everything they had."*

A Spirit-led life also propels believers to act as a conduit of God's love through kindness, goodness, and faithfulness. Such acts of virtue, fueled by a sincere devotion to divine principles, cultivate an atmosphere where the **fruits of the Holy Spirit freely blossom**. (Tarrants, 2016). Members of the community are inspired to emulate these behaviors, creating a ripple effect that deepens faith and unity, transforming not just the individual but the whole community. Regular engagement in community activities, such as helping those in need or participating in group worship, bolsters unity and highlights the significance of living under the Spirit's guidance. (How the Holy Spirit Can Ignite Your Ordinary Life, 2015). These experiences serve as tangible demonstrations of love and cooperation, illustrating the profound impact of living in harmony with the Spirit. **Galatians 5:22-23** reminds us, *"But the fruit of the Spirit is love, joy, peace, forbearance, kindness, goodness, faithfulness, gentleness and self-control. Against such things there is no law."*

When individuals fully commit to a Spirit-led existence, their lives become testimonials of faith and transformation. These personal stories, shared among believers, become potential catalysts for reviving others' faltering spirits or encouraging those who stand at the boundaries of their faith. Take, for example, a believer's decision to escape the cycle of sin and addiction. Through the Spirit's influence, they find newfound strength and liberation, stepping into a life of obedience and discipline that eventually enriches both their personal journey and the faith community at large. (Tarrants, 2016).

2 Corinthians 5:17 states, *"Therefore, if anyone is in Christ, the new creation has come: The old has gone, the new is here!"* - *NIV*

The Spirit also plays a crucial role in fostering discernment among believers. It's about honing the ability to distinguish between secular desires and spiritual motivations to align personal goals with divine mandates. This spiritual wisdom allows believers to pursue endeavors that ultimately support the collective mission—be it through church-related projects or general acts of service that reflect godly values. Daily challenges become opportunities to practice discernment, as believers train themselves to pause, pray, and ponder before making decisions, inviting the Spirit to light the path forward. **Proverbs 3:5-6** advises, *"Trust in the Lord with all your heart and lean not on your own understanding; in all your ways submit to him, and he will make your paths straight."*

Building on this foundation, living a Spirit-led life is a call to proactive faith, where believers step beyond mere contemplation of possibilities to take tangible action. With the Spirit as their guide, believers embark on ventures that are not just beneficial for personal growth but also advance the kingdom of God. Through these actions, they cultivate spaces for learning and relational growth, enhancing their community's spiritual ecosystem. (How the Holy Spirit Can Ignite Your Ordinary Life, 2015). Propelled by the Spirit's energy, members of the faith community animate the grace that flows within them, challenging inhibition and inspiring bold, faith-driven initiatives. **James 1:22** encourages, *"Do not merely listen to the word, and so deceive yourselves. Do what it says."*

Interestingly, the Spirit's influence extends to reshaping perspectives, allowing individuals to embrace purpose and understanding where there once was confusion and hesitation. Recognizing the inclusive and empowering nature of the Spirit's presence, believers harness this energy as a focal point in addressing their fears, insecurities, and uncertainties. With each hurdle overcome, they cultivate a resilience that not only strengthens their own faith but also emboldens others within their community.

Spirit-led living transforms personal and communal dynamics into a divine tapestry of purpose, harmony, and zeal for advancing God's kingdom. By leveraging each person's unique gifts in alignment with divine guidance, believers collectively bring forth a narrative of faith that pulses with life and vitality. Their shared mission transcends individual pursuits, weaving a sprawling network of faith and purpose, empowered by the Spirit to reflect God's glory in myriad ways. As they walk this path with intentionality and commitment, believers illuminate a world often shadowed by doubt, offering a beacon of hope that leads back to the heart of God. Through ongoing engagement and intentional community building, the Holy Spirit's influence manifests visibly and persistently in the lives of those who dare to venture into the Spirit-led journey.

Summary and Reflections

Understanding the vital role of **spiritual unity** and collective purpose leads us to realize the **incredible potential** within a closely-knit community of believers. By embracing this unity, we pave the way for more profound collaboration in fulfilling God's mission as **His Royal family**. This chapter has highlighted how shared experiences, such as baptisms and testimonies, foster strong bonds and mutual support among believers. These connections not only enrich our individual faith journeys but also enhance the Church's ability to serve the world with love and compassion. Now that we've grasped these foundational elements, we can look ahead to how they empower us in collaborative missions under the Spirit's guidance. As you continue your spiritual journey, embracing this unity and spirit-led lifestyle will equip you to engage more fully with your faith community, enriching your own spiritual growth and contributing significantly to building **God's kingdom on earth**. Amen.

José E. Espinoza

<u>Conclusion</u>

As you stand at the threshold of your new journey with God, it's important to recognize the foundation on which every thriving relationship with Him is built: **genuine <u>Adoration/worship</u>**. True Adoration/worship isn't limited to a church service or a set of rituals; it's about meeting God personally and letting that encounter shape who you are and how you live each day. When you approach worship with authenticity—**<u>honestly seeking God</u>** rather than simply following routines—<u>you open yourself to transformation</u>. This kind of worship makes room for real change within, allowing faith to grow beyond surface-level practices into a living, breathing part of your identity.

Worship also lays the groundwork for deep connection to God through prayer. **PRAYER** is so much more than reciting words—it's an ongoing conversation, **<u>a vital link between you and your Creator</u>**. In moments of joy, pain, confusion, or hope, <u>prayer invites God into every part of your</u>

story. With each honest prayer, your spiritual resilience grows. Even when life feels overwhelming or uncertain, turning to God in prayer brings peace and perspective. The storms do not disappear, but you discover strength and calm as you align yourself with His presence and purpose.

The choices you make every day are opportunities to put God's priorities first. Adopting a Kingdom mindset means asking, "How can I reflect God's love right now?" It's about filtering decisions—not just the big ones, but even small, daily actions—through the lens of God's values. When you prioritize the things that matter most to God, your life starts to look different. You become someone who serves others, reaches out to those in need, and finds meaning beyond personal achievement. Living this way sharpens your sense of calling and anchors your purpose, reminding you that faith is never meant to be private or passive.

Yet, adopting this new way of life comes with **challenges**. Distractions will inevitably compete for your attention—whether it's internal doubts, outside pressures, old habits, or unexpected setbacks. It's easy to get sidetracked or discouraged when your intentions collide with reality. But overcoming these obstacles is crucial. Recognize what pulls your focus away from God. Take active steps to refocus—setting aside time for prayer, being honest about your struggles, and surrounding yourself with people who encourage your growth. By doing so, you nurture perseverance, making it possible to sustain your faith even when life gets hard.

At the heart of Christian living lies a commitment to the **authority of the <u>BIBLE</u>**. <u>The Scriptures</u> aren't just ancient writings—they're **<u>God's ongoing message to humanity</u>**. <u>Trusting the Bible as your guide</u> shapes your worldview, influences your choices, and <u>helps you discern right from wrong</u>. Taking the Bible in your heart, as God's own words to you and for you: You'll find wisdom for difficult situations and guidance for everyday questions as you read and reflect on its truths. Embracing the authority of Scripture anchors you during uncertain times and propels you forward, challenging you to move beyond comfort zones and pursue a deeper obedience.

Within its pages, **the Bible also offers promises** that stand as unshakable pillars throughout life's changes. These promises remind you that you are never alone—that God's character is steadfast, and His plans are for your good. When you face doubt or hardship, holding onto God's promises gives you reason to hope, even if circumstances don't immediately improve. Let these assurances cultivate trust, drive away fear, and fill you with courage to keep walking the path of faith.

More than anything, Christianity calls you to experience and express God's unconditional love. Understanding this love is transformative—not just in how you see yourself, but in how you relate to others. God's love empowers you to forgive, reach out, show patience, and act with kindness— even when it feels costly or inconvenient. As you embrace and embody divine love, relationships deepen, and communities grow stronger. Love becomes your motivation, fueling acts of compassion and making faith visible through service, generosity, and empathy.

A life shaped by faith will naturally hunger for justice. Seeking justice means advocating for fairness, standing alongside the marginalized, and choosing mercy over indifference. The call to justice isn't reserved for the few—it's woven into the fabric of every believer's walk with God. Pursue justice daily: speak up for those without a voice, challenge unfairness where you find it, and be quick to offer forgiveness rather than judgment. Justice, anchored in God's character, transforms families, neighborhoods, and entire communities as you reflect His heart for all people.

Entering the Kingdom of God is not just a one-time event, but <u>the beginning of an ongoing spiritual awakening</u>. This awakening deepens as you intentionally seek God's presence and take steps like baptism—a tangible sign of your commitment to Him and an invitation for the Holy Spirit to work more powerfully in your life. Baptism is both a symbol and a launching point; it marks a new chapter where your relationship with God is strengthened and your awareness of His work in your life grows clearer each day.

Yet, coming to faith is only the starting line. The path ahead is called discipleship—a lifelong process of learning, growing, and following Jesus' example. **Discipleship** involves consistent reflection on <u>Scripture</u>, regular <u>prayer</u>, and participation in a loving <u>community</u> that keeps you accountable and encouraged. Every moment spent learning, serving, and listening draws you closer to God's heart and molds you into someone who reflects Christ in word and deed. Real growth happens as you invite feedback, ask hard questions, and practice faithfulness even when it requires sacrifice.

Central to this journey is the call to share your faith boldly. Jesus invites every believer to be part of bringing the good news to others. **The Holy Spirit** empowers you to speak with clarity, humility, and confidence—not because you have all the answers, but because you've experienced **the transforming power of the Gospel** firsthand. Your story, no matter how simple or complicated, can make an eternal difference for someone searching for hope. Don't underestimate the ripple effect of your witness; every conversation, act of kindness, and shared testimony has the potential to draw others toward a relationship with Christ.

Finally, remember the gift of **spiritual unity**. The Church is meant to be a family—diverse, yet united in purpose and mission. Within this community, your unique gifts are valued, and your struggles are carried together. When believers celebrate differences, support one another, and pool resources and prayers, the impact multiplies far beyond what any one person could achieve alone. **Unity in Christ** fortifies you against isolation, encourages mutual accountability, and testifies powerfully to the world about the love of God.

As you step forward, know that building a meaningful relationship with God rests on sincere **adoration**/worship, heartfelt **prayer**, alignment with **His Kingdom**, an unwavering commitment to Scripture's truth; **The Bible**, and lastly but not least; Connected in/to **The Holy Spirit**. Lean on God's promises when uncertainty arises, allow His love to reshape your interactions, seek justice wherever you find need, and let your life be marked by acts of faith and bold **sharing of the Evangelical Message**. Engage fully in your faith community, making room for both accountability and celebration, as together you grow in unity and purpose.

The journey ahead will hold moments of challenge and wonder, failure and triumph. Through it all, remember: God is at work in you and through you, equipping you to live with purpose, courage, and grace. Embrace every opportunity to draw near to Him, knowing that each step taken in faith brings you closer to the abundant life He desires for you.

THE END.

José E. Espinoza

BLESSINGS

&

Welcome to Being Part

Of

The Citizenship of

The Kingdom of God

Through <u>Jesus Christ</u>; Lord & Savior

Amen.

-   José E. Espinoza

About The Author

José E. Espinoza is a writer, instructor, and Christian guide specializing in **leadership** and personal development for young adults, experienced individuals, and professionals. He has been a dedicated **missionary** since his youth, consistently committed to sharing the evangelical message of **The Kingdom of God**.

José E. Espinoza

Other books from The Author

Message of Jesus #1

Proclamation of the Kingdom of Heaven on Earth as Primary Objective

Priority #1

How your Primary Purpose Takes Preeminence

TIME, TALENT, TREASURE

Human Life equation

Awareness for a Meaningful Life Existence

www.ingramcontent.com/pod-product-compliance
Lightning Source LLC
Chambersburg PA
CBHW051957090426
42741CB00008B/1434